Buddha's Book
of Stress Reduction

WITHDRAWN

JOSEPH EMET

TARCHER/PENGUIN

a member of Penguin Group (USA)

New York

Buddha's Book of Stress Reduction

Finding Serenity and Peace with

Mindfulness Meditation

JEREMY P. TARCHER/PENGUIN
Published by the Penguin Group
Penguin Group (USA) LLC
375 Hudson Street
New York, New York 10014

USA · Canada · UK · Ireland · Australia
New Zealand · India · South Africa · China

penguin.com
A Penguin Random House Company

Copyright © 2013 by Joseph Emet
Penguin supports copyright. Copyright fuels creativity, encourages diverse voices,
promotes free speech, and creates a vibrant culture. Thank you for buying an authorized
edition of this book and for complying with copyright laws by not reproducing, scanning,
or distributing any part of it in any form without permission. You are supporting writers
and allowing Penguin to continue to publish books for every reader.

Most Tarcher/Penguin books are available at special quantity discounts for bulk purchase for sales
promotions, premiums, fund-raising, and educational needs. Special books or book excerpts also
can be created to fit specific needs. For details, write: Special.Markets@us.penguingroup.com.

Some of the names and identifying characteristics of the people featured in this
book have been changed to protect their privacy.

Library of Congress Cataloging-in-Publication

Emet, Joseph.
Buddha's book of stress reduction : finding serenity and peace with mindfulness meditation / Joseph Emet.
p.   cm.
ISBN 978-0-399-16733-1
1. Stress (Psychology)—Religious aspects—Buddhism.   2. Spiritual life—Buddhism.   3. Stress management.   I. Title.
BQ4570.S77E64   2013   2013037079
294.3'4435—dc23

Printed in the United States of America
1   3   5   7   9   10   8   6   4   2

Book design by Gretchen Achilles

Neither the publisher nor the author is engaged in rendering professional advice or services to
the individual reader. The ideas, procedures, and suggestions contained in this book are not
intended as a substitute for consulting with your physician. All matters regarding your health
require medical supervision. Neither the author nor the publisher shall be liable or responsible
for any loss or damage allegedly arising from any information or suggestion in this book.

Dedicated to Thich Nhat Hanh, with gratitude and heartfelt thanks

for the gift of mindfulness, for transmitting Buddha's presence as well as his words,

for underlining such essentials as love and happiness,

and for opening the doors of poetry and music

for so many of us

Contents

PART ONE
The Mind

PART TWO

Control and Acceptance

PART THREE

Change

Foreword

Mindfulness is a child of the Buddha.

This book presents mindfulness teachings in a practical way, with exercises that show us how to apply them in various areas of everyday living. Knowing how to be mindful in everyday life is an art, the art of mindful living. Stress is a pervasive challenge of our time, and when we live mindfully, we live with awareness of the roots of stress in ourselves and in our society. Once we recognize the roots of stress, it is easier to live without allowing stress to destroy our happiness and our health.

May this book be a step on your journey into the art of mindful living.

—*Thich Nhat Hanh*
Plum Village, France

Introduction

If you think of stress as one problem among many, please consider the following:

Major psychological challenges such as burnout, depression, and anxiety all have a stress component, and burnout in particular is thought to be caused directly by excessive and prolonged stress.

Stress contributes to accidents and to suicide as well as to illnesses that are the primary causes of death, such as heart disease, cancer, lung diseases, and cirrhosis of the liver. Because it interferes with the functioning of the immune system, it aggravates most infectious diseases.

It is a factor in sexual disorders and in conjugal violence, and it erodes relationships. It fuels addictions and substance abuse. It aggravates sleep problems.

Perhaps in recognition of its import, some prominent translators of Buddhist texts now often render the key Buddhist word "Dukkha"—which is usually translated as "suffering"—as "stress."

◆ ◆ ◆

This book proposes to take you all the way from stress to well-being.

It starts by making you aware of how you are creating extra stress in your life with your attitude and your reactions. No, it is not all in your head: life is stressful, and some lives more so than others, and different people react to similar situations differently. Yet there is a part of stress that *is* in your head. That is the part that all stress books address because that is the part that you *can* control. Recognizing the difference between what we can control and what we can't is crucial for stress management—and is a sort of awakening in itself. Are you barking up the wrong tree, the tree of other people and what they are doing? Are you spending your energy wishing that others would change their ways? If so, change trees, because this will only serve to tire you out. Become more aware of your own reactions to things, and how your reactions contribute to your stress. Come back to your own tree and take care of it. Enjoy its shade and its fruits. You will get more out of life that way. This book shows you how to achieve this with a series of exercises at the end of each chapter. Some of these exercises are guided meditations and some are meditation themes.

As much as stress constricts our field of vision, a relaxed attitude and good feelings broaden it.

As much as stress is associated with negative emotions like fear and anger, well-being is linked with positive emotions like love, inspiration, and serenity.

As much as stress tends to act like blinders so that we see only the negative side of events and circumstances, positive feelings expand our perspective so we see a more complete picture that takes account of the good things as well—which are everywhere around us, in the blue sky, in the bloom of flowers, and in the joy of simply being alive.

As much as stress makes us aware of possible danger, positive emotions take stock of opportunity. A direct result of this is that stress can get us stuck in inaction, whereas positive emotions like hope, inspiration, and interest help propel us forward toward success.

And last but not least, as much as stress is associated with ill health and a shortened lifespan, research shows that positive feelings improve our health and make us live longer.

If stress is one side of the coin, well-being is the other—literally. While one side of most coins may have only numbers (the bottom line), the other side has a human face, a natural symbol, or a reminder of our national heritage—a broader vision of life. Stress is woven into the fabric of our life, and in order to reduce how much stress we feel, we need to examine all aspects of our life. During this process, we gain more intimacy with ourselves and more wisdom. This, in turn, brings a sense of well-being and contentment. Stress reduction can lead to growth if done right, and to do it right we need to keep in mind that our goal is not only moving away from stress, but also moving forward toward well-being.

Positive feelings of joy and gratitude are themselves an antidote to stress. In addition, as discussed in chapter 6, living by values that are personally important to us leads to fulfillment and a sense of well-being. Values influence our actions in the present moment. In contrast, goals are in the future. The pressure to achieve goals may bring extra stress. Living by cherished values brings contentment.

Stress is made up of many elements—things with names like Worry, Irritation, Anger, Fear, and Difficult Relationships. It also has much to do with the way we think. Many of these issues are discussed in separate chapters in this book.

We all need the mindfulness mantra: BE HERE NOW. We all have the ability to be in our thoughts, instead of with the person we are with. We all can be mentally somewhere else instead of enjoying life as it unfolds in and around us. Mindfulness meditation training helps us all to moderate these common habits and lead a happier life.

Sometimes it is a difficult childhood or a childhood trauma that prevents us from being fully present. When we have indigestion, we are still trying to digest last night's meal in the morning. Similarly, when we have past wounds, we may still be licking them now. That keeps a part of us *there*, instead of *here*.

◆ ◆ ◆

When we need to feel better, we may reach for alcohol, drugs, or food. They are available off the shelf, and their effects are direct and immediate. These effects, however, also disappear quickly. They do not lead to long-term change.

Consider this: if you try to make yourself feel better with a few beers, you are still on square one at the end of the day. After a day of mindfulness practice, you are now on square two. And the effects of mindfulness practice continue to add up. After a year of distractions, you are still on square one, whereas after a year of mindfulness practice, you are now on square 365—a much better place to be! Distractions may have their place, but they do not give you self-knowledge and freedom from the tyranny of automatic thoughts.

There are many books on stress—a whole stress literature. There is also a well-being or happiness literature. This book straddles the two areas. My aim in writing this book has been to bring these two fields together and show how they are related. Learning to go from stress toward well-being is a major thrust of the Buddhist tradition, a teaching that I absorbed during my training in mindfulness practice with the Zen master Thich Nhat Hanh. I emphasize this forward-looking approach in my own stress-reduction classes, and I would like to bring this important teaching to you with this book. I call this process Mindfulness Training for Stress Reduction and Personal Growth. The relationship between these two goals will become clearer as you make your way through the book.

◆

PART ONE

The Mind

1.

The Stress Blues

A baby smiles between fifty and seventy times a day, and a toddler approximately
six hundred times, according to research. I'm sure some of us have asked
ourselves where that smile goes. What robs us of it?

—GOLDIE HAWN, *10 Mindful Minutes*

An easy smile is one of the first things that disappear as we get stressed. When we were children, we smiled a lot because we lived in the present moment. We had the "here and now" mind. Life's simple joys were enough to delight us. But growing up involves learning to give up that "here and now" mind in favor of the tomorrow mind, the future mind. The future can be a source of purpose: the toddler who is just playing with his shoelaces instead of putting on his shoes, or playing hide-and-seek using his shirt as a prop instead of getting dressed, as his mom wants him to, is in the present. He is having fun because he does not see beyond the present. He does not have an agenda or a to-do list for the afternoon like his mom does. A purpose changes our focus from the present to the future. And when we are doing *everything* with a purpose in mind, the present disappears.

How many times were we urged by our parents to do that as we were growing up?

How many times a day?

Mindfulness practice can help us find that smile and bring it back to our hearts and minds. It can bring the smile back into our lives.

Smiling relaxes. A true smile comes from the heart and radiates out to the whole body, softening and healing every part.

Find Your Smile Again

Try it now. Close your eyes for a minute and visualize a smile opening in your heart, like a flower opens its petals as it blooms. After you hold that blossom in your heart, visualize it spreading out like spring flowers to every part of your body. The smile on your face comes when the flowers arrive there. This is a body scan with flowers! Now try to keep the flowers as you open your eyes. Doesn't the world look different?

"Smile, life's a miracle," says Thich Nhat Hanh. Lose yourself again in that miracle like you once did as a child. You are that miracle. Feeling life from the inside is a true miracle. (A body scan is a guided meditation practice designed to cultivate awareness of body sensations and concentration. You can find many body scans of different lengths on YouTube by searching for "body scan meditation.")

Some people take to this teaching like a thirsty person takes to a glass of cool water. They know the "parched" feeling that comes from not being able to enjoy the moment because they are always thinking about the next thing or planning for tomorrow. They have known what it feels like to do chores all day and toil without ever reaping the reward, the reward that is enjoying the present moment. The present moment is always there, but they are not there to enjoy it. They have always been thinking of tomorrow. The reward never comes for them. Living like that is like collecting discount coupons and never cashing them in.

Others are skeptical. They have learned to make a virtue out of planning for the future. They do not want tomorrow to come and find themselves unprepared. They toil stoically because it is the "right thing to do." They even look askance at people who take time to enjoy themselves—they see these people as lacking in some kind of moral fiber.

You know the child's mind, and you also know the mother's mind. You know that the child lives in a different world, where tomorrow never comes—it is always today. Charming, but also frustrating! Work must be done, and groceries must be bought. Yet you are now at this impasse where you feel the stress, and your joie de vivre is evaporating.

I am not proposing that we throw away our adult life skills. Those hard-earned skills have their place. I am proposing that we stop systematically throwing away the present moment. Living in the past or the future has become a habit for many of us. We even continue to do it when we are resting or on vacation. Indeed, for some, a scheduled rest time may even be more stressful than work. At least when we are engaged in work, our mind is not obsessing about the past or worrying about the future. Work is a way to keep the mind engaged in the present. When that pressure lifts, you may experience more stress instead of less. All of a sudden your mind has nothing to do, and without some training in enjoying the present moment (just what the mother tried so hard to train the child not to do), you may find that now you have nothing to enjoy. You are instead more stressed, thinking more about the future, or rethinking past actions. Indeed, many people find retirement a particularly stressful time, as I discuss later. Many others find vacations stressful. Both of those times are about now, not about the future.

The Now Mind

Being in the moment is one of the fundamentals of mindfulness practice.

However, this teaching appears to go against the current of the Protestant ethic, which emphasizes hard work and toil *now*, and enjoyment of success (perhaps) *later*. In this worldview, having fun and enjoying the moment has often been seen as a moral failing.

Yet life is only available in the present, and the Protestant work ethic itself can be a source of stress.

We can't live in the past or the future except in our minds. And when we do live in our minds, we find it difficult to relax. Not only is life available only in the present, but so is rest.

Be Here Now and Rest Your Mind

Without mindfulness, rest may not be available when you make time for it. Your mind might still be going, worrying about something or other or fussing about an upsetting event that happened yesterday. Your mind may be reliving that upset over and over again and flooding your body with the same stress hormones that it produced during the actual event.

"Truly I tell you, unless you change and become like little children, you will never enter the kingdom of heaven."

That precious verse from the Book of Matthew says it all. Thich Nhat Hanh adds that the kingdom of heaven is NOW. NOW is our home, and being in the present moment allows the mind to rest.

Mindfulness practice gives us a chance to get in touch with our breath and our body, and through them, encounter the present moment. We get relief from tomorrow-mind, and from yesterday-mind. We learn to find joy in today-mind.

With mindfulness, *we* are in charge of our mind and of our life, not the habits that have been drilled into us. In fact, those habits are not the culprits. They have made it possible for us to be successful in school and at work. The stress comes from fusing with this habit so completely that we lose our precious freedom. Without mindfulness we *become* our habits.

◆

Smiling!

You can smile four times an hour during the rest of the day. If you enjoy the results, you can do it tomorrow as well.

It's worth remembering this slightly amended version of a common saying: "A journey of a thousand smiles begins with the first smile." That first smile could be the fifst smile of a day, the first smile of a conversation, or, more in line with the original saying, the first smile of a car trip. The first smile is an important one, for it can change the course of a day or the tone of a conversation.

You can help smiles happen more frequently by posting SMILE signs as reminders.

2.

Two Kinds of Thinking

There's nothing more important to true growth than realizing that you
are not the voice of the mind—you are the one who hears it.
—MICHAEL A. SINGER

We may say, "You think too much," to someone who seems preoccupied or worried, or who looks like they are lost in thought. But I can't imagine that a death row inmate ever said that to his lawyer. You would not consider saying that to your tax consultant or to your doctor. We want these people to think, and we pay them to do it.

But we pay them to think in a certain way, with a purpose, and for our benefit. Two different kinds of activity go under the name "thinking." Sometimes we think with a purpose in mind, and sometimes our thinking happens automatically—it can even occur below our awareness. We may also take our automatic thoughts as representing the way things are and not question them. Understanding the way we think is the key to understanding how we create our own stress as well as our own well-being. Because thinking is such an important part of stress, I start this book by taking a close look at this all-pervasive activity.

Automatic Thoughts and Stress

Laurie worked in a large office dealing with people on welfare. Her work included field visits to her clients. Lately, one of her superiors had been asking other people in the office where Laurie was when she was out, and making oblique references to her frequent absences from the office. There was nothing out in the open, no confrontation of any kind, but nevertheless Laurie found the situation quite stressful.

I asked her what she was telling herself about the situation. "He does not trust me," she said. I asked if that was a purposeful, realistic evaluation. After some discussion, it became clear that it was an automatic thought on her part. The supervisor did that to other people as well. Laurie's stress was caused not so much by what her superior was doing, but by what she was telling herself—automatically. The supervisor was just doing his job.

This confusion between what is actually happening and the story we tell ourselves about it is quite common. Once we recognize that we are creating most of our own stress (with a little help from others), it is easier to deal with it. But that first step of recognition can be elusive.

I asked Laurie about the interactions she had with her welfare clients. Did they cause her stress? "No," she said. She was glad to be of help. Indeed, she was a helpful kind of person by nature—she exuded a "How can I help you?" kind of manner when she spoke. She spent several hours each day with her clients, and only a few minutes each week with her supervisor. Yet those few minutes created more stress. She did not ruminate about her meetings with her clients after the meetings were over. She was able to turn the page and move on. But she played back the conversations with her supervisor over and over again in her mind.

I asked her to be mindful of the stories she told herself around those meetings with her supervisor. How were those stories different from the stories she told herself about her clients? As we talked, it became clear that with her clients, her mind was in a problem-solving mode. With her supervisor, she switched into an automatic thinker.

All Thinking Is Not the Same

We owe much of our success, both as a species and as individuals, to our thinking. But we owe much of our misery to it as well.

Purposive thinking and automatic thinking are quite different in character. Purposive thinking can make us successful and wealthy. It can keep us out of trouble. Automatic thinking can make us stressed and anxious. It can get us into trouble.

In purposive thinking we control the process. Doing our income tax, studying for an exam, and solving a problem are examples of purposive thinking. It makes it possible for a doctor to diagnose a patient, a lawyer to prepare her case, and a plumber to figure out a problem. I am using purposive thinking now to write this book. (For the very important role that inspiration plays in creativity, see chapter 4.) In purposive thinking we control the agenda. *We* decide what is important, *we* decide what to research, and *we* draw the conclusions. *We* are in charge. We use the thinking mind to suit our own purposes, much like we use a computer. Our computer does not choose what documents to open, who to send messages to, and what to write in an e-mail (except when it has been hijacked).

A mind in the automatic-thinking mode behaves like a hijacked computer. It has been hijacked by emotions or a wild imagination. In automatic thinking we are not in charge. The mind serves us the thoughts it wants.

One could also compare automatic thoughts to the unsolicited flyers that clutter the mailbox or advertisements on the radio. The only difference is that automatic thoughts come from inside us rather than from the outside. And that creates a recognition problem: we believe our automatic thoughts and we identify with them because they are said in our own voice.

Automatic Thinking Just Happens

The mind is a good servant, but it can be a poor master.

At best, automatic thoughts are irrelevant—they rehash past experiences or they are daydreams about the future. Even then they take us away from the moment: while we are daydreaming, we may be missing the exit we need to take, or we miss a chance to connect with the person we are with. We do what we are doing halfheartedly because the other half of our mind is taken up with automatic thoughts.

But there is a darker side to automatic thinking. The mind can be taken over by fears and anxiety, or by greed and cravings. If we are prone to depression, the mind keeps playing the same MP3 track about hard times and bad karma. If we are prone to anxiety, it plays the song about the monsters in the closet over and over again. No problem is solved, and this "free entertainment" is not getting any laughs. On the contrary, our stress level goes up, and our comfort level goes down.

Automatic thinking broadcasts on the same frequency as problem solving. Its voice sounds familiar: it's our voice. And it can be detrimental—the thinking process that we trust because it brings us benefits has now been hijacked and lost its purpose. It has been commandeered by the lords of fear and anxiety. We listen trustingly, and we suffer. Sometimes there is only blabber and no goal. Then, these messages can be just irrelevant. But they can also be harmful, as when they tell us that everything is going wrong when that is not true.

The Two Faces of Thinking

The mind can be a confusing place! These two faces of thinking are a bit like the two masks of the drama symbol—the smiling face and the weeping face. That symbol for the theater comes to us from ancient Greece, where actors played multiple roles in the same play, and they put on masks to show a change of character or of mood. In the theater of the mind, our mind changes from purposive thinker to automatic thinker without changing masks and without letting us know. Without mindfulness, we may not be able to see the difference. Thus a competent person can solve other people's problems all day long at work using purposive thinking. Then she can go home and become prey to spontaneous thoughts and suffer from depression. This is a real problem for psychologists: a 2009 American Psychological Association survey found that 40 percent to 60 percent of psychological practitioners reported some disruption in professional functioning due to burnout, anxiety, or depression. This is a huge percentage, especially among specialists who seemingly should know better. Without mindfulness, the very feeling of competence may play tricks on us. Competence may increase our confidence in the thinking process: after all, we use our thinking at work and see how effective it can be. We are encouraged to trust our mind without question, and may be more likely to believe our own thoughts.

A psychological practitioner, however, is competent only as long as she is using purposive thinking. Her automatic thoughts are just as suspect as anyone else's automatic thoughts, including her clients'. When she fuses with them and identifies with them, she is on slippery ground because she is no longer using her field of competence. After all, she did not get her degree using automatic thinking, she got it using purposive thinking. What would a term paper that consisted only of your automatic thoughts look like? How would a professor receive it?

Two Faces of Worrying

Just like thinking, worrying also has two faces. A cognitive worry goes away when you take care of what's causing it. An automatically arising emotional worry doesn't. Is your worry a cognitive kind of worry that is based on reason, and are you dealing with it in a rational way, by taking preventive and proactive measures that make sense? Or is it an emotional kind of worry that refuses to go away no matter what you do? Purposive thinking can solve cognitive worries: we set out to analyze the situation, discover appropriate remedies, and apply them.

Here's an example: lately your brakes are not working well and you begin to worry that someday you may get into an accident. You go to a mechanic and get a brake job. Problem solved, worry gone.

Emotional worries are more complicated. For starters, the cause of the worry is inside the worrier. Outside circumstances are mostly triggers that activate this worrying nature. Such a person is sometimes described as a worrywart—a description that points the finger clearly at the worrying person rather than at the circumstances. Automatic thinking fuels the flames of this kind of worry, and emotion is the wind that makes the flames grow wild and spread.

Effective Thinking and Mindfulness

There are many books on effective thinking. These books discuss how to improve our *purposive* thinking. A competent worker, however, may already have effective thinking skills: she uses them all day long at work as she solves the many problems she encounters. But she may not be able to do for herself what she does well for others. She is using purposive thinking to help others. But she may be using her automatic thoughts as she contemplates her own life.

We can improve our purposive thinking by going to school, learning a trade, or learning effective thinking skills.

But how do we get a handle on our automatic thinking? When automatic thinking is bringing us anxiety, depression, or stress, it is having an effect on our quality of life. This effect can be as big in a negative way as the positive effect of a college degree. In some cases it can be even bigger. Mindfulness is a key skill for learning to manage our automatic thoughts.

Awareness of Automatic Thoughts

When a competent person is thinking purposively, she knows it. If she is a lawyer, she may be billing her clients for every minute of it. Purposive thinking is something she can turn on.

By contrast, automatic thinking sneaks up on us. It comes unbidden and uninvited.

We may not even be aware that it is happening. We have been living with it since childhood. It is like the proverbial fish not being aware of the water it is swimming in.

Swimming Meditation for Fish

Cultivating the habit of being aware of automatic thoughts is like teaching a fish to become aware that it is swimming in water.

The fish may have to practice swimming awareness—be aware of all the sensations of swimming, how the fins push against something, what happens during breathing, during floating, so that awareness slowly builds up, and one day it explodes into insight. Then the fish may understand many of the puzzles that come with living in water.

Just Idling in Neutral

When you buy a car with a big engine, it not only performs big, but it idles big as well. This is also true of the human brain. The human brain is large compared to the brains of most other animals. It performs powerfully, solving the mysteries of physics and tax forms, but it also idles with much noise and smoke. Our automatic thoughts and worries are that noise and smoke. Perhaps in prehistoric times, that large brain was kept busy with problems of survival in a wild world. It was thinking purposefully much of the time to find food and shelter. Actually, not too long ago, many Inuit in the "Grand Nord" of Québec lived in igloos, used whale oil lamps for light in the long and dark winter months, melted snow to make drinking water, and wore homemade animal-skin clothes and mukluks. Just think of the difficulties of taking care of babies under those conditions. The typical urban apartment dweller does not face the same kind of constant survival problems. Her brain is idling much of the time.

The Stress Pyramid

Mindfulness meditation brings understanding, clarity, and awareness to the mind. The natural tendency of the mind is to look outside. We evolved in a dangerous world of prey and predator. Our ancestors needed to be constantly on the lookout—either to make sure that they did not become another predator's lunch, or to make sure that they got some lunch for themselves. Humans are often portrayed as the tip of the evolutionary pyramid. But we are also the tip of the stress pyramid. Fish experience physical stress when conditions are not right for them. But they do not worry about hypothetical dangers in the future or fret about things like not realizing their full career potential. Humans are experts at that. We experience physical stressors like other animals. But we also experience a host of extra psychological stressors of which animals are blissfully unaware. For humans, such psychological stress factors are added on to physical stressors. It's the price we pay for our place at the top of the evolution pyramid.

Looking In

In mindfulness meditation we bring the mind to look *inside* with a scientific attitude of observation and acceptance. Again and again the mind's centrifugal tendency wins out, and it turns its gaze outside. Or it loses its focus and, instead of observing, it daydreams. We, in turn, bring the mind back to look inward again as an observer. This is not something we can do once and for all. We have to do it over and over, because the mind constantly slips away from our intention.

Lately the 10,000 hour rule has become a popular paradigm for learning a skill as a result of Malcolm Gladwell's 2008 book, *Outliers: The Story of Success*. Gladwell stresses the hard work and the time it takes to master a skill. However, take heart: we do not have to wait until we become a Buddha in order to taste the fruits of mindfulness practice. Every gain we make in awareness brings rewards, because it decreases our stress and increases our freedom.

Incidentally, freedom has a specific meaning in Buddhism. It means having choices over our attitudes and behavior. When we are not free we act out of habit, or react to emotional impulses or to cravings and aversions without thought. There is no freedom in a knee-jerk reflex. Without mindfulness, a good part of our behavior is automatic like that. People and situations "push our buttons," and we act in predictable ways. As we become proficient in developing the observer attitude of mindfulness, we learn to observe our cravings, aversions, and emotional impulses without being compelled by them.

"I Don't Think I'm Doing It Right"

The meditating Buddha looks so effortless and natural. Many people measure their meditation practice by it and find that they come up short. Their own experience of meditation is not so easy and natural. They become frustrated and conclude that they are doing it wrong.

The Buddha depicted in those pictures and statues, however, was not a beginner. In the beginning, you get in touch with your breath, and a few moments later find that your mind is elsewhere. You get in touch with the five senses and stay on track while you are being guided through a body scan. But as soon as the instructions stop, you lose your focus and find yourself in the middle of a daydream. The drifting mind and the daydream are not meditation. But coming back over and over and intentionally paying attention to your inner experience is part of the practice. Beware of perfectionism. Concentration does not necessarily mean perfect, absolute concentration. There is a well-known line in Leonard Cohen's song "Anthem": "There is a crack in everything, that's how the light gets in." That's how the thought that "it is time to stop meditating and do something else" also gets in—through a crack in your concentration. Otherwise you may be stuck in meditation until you die!

But a crack in the wall is quite different from not having a wall at all.

Without a wall, you are at the mercy of rain, snow, and the cold wind. At the beginning of meditation practice, the crack might be wide. Not only the light, but also many kinds of distracting thoughts find their way in. By the time the crack is only a small breach in your concentration, you are doing well.

You Can't Manage Stress with the Stress Habit!

When we turn meditation into another task that we want to do perfectly, it becomes a performance. It can even be another source of stress! Don't let the word "concentration" put you into the doing-mode. Meditation is a form of not-doing—not daydreaming, not wanting things to be otherwise, and not struggling with your mind. Just being—being the observer. Concentration, as used in this context, means the ability to keep this observer stance going.

Say that you are working in a fruit-packing plant and your job is to observe apples moving on a conveyor belt. If you get carried away by the looks of a certain apple, reach for it, and take a bite, you have lost it—you are no longer just the observer. In a similar way, when you get carried away by a thought and start identifying with it instead of just observing it, you have lost your concentration. You have taken a bite. Gently notice what happened and just come back to your breath. You will need to do this over and over again, without frustration, and preferably while smiling to yourself: you are an apple addict now in charge of just observing them moving along! Occasional transgressions are inevitable at the beginning, and nothing to fret about. We are all thought addicts.

Thoughts Are Not Only in the Mind

When we think words, our speaking muscles and vocal cords are slightly activated. This finding gave rise to speed-reading—in speed-reading we scan a line quickly, at a speed that makes it impossible to think of individual words. Normally, as we read a word we also subvocalize. Our speaking muscles are activated very lightly. This slows down reading because then we can only read at the speed we talk, and not at the speed we can think.

There are computerized mechanical limbs for handicapped people based on the same principle. They transform signals from the brain into ordinary electric signals that activate a mechanical device. You can raise a bionic arm just by thinking of raising your arm. Jesse Sullivan, the world's first bionic man, uses such a prosthesis. In May 2001, while working as a high-power electrical lineman, Sullivan was so severely shot through with electric current that both of his arms had to be amputated. He was then fitted with a mechanical arm that can read the nerve impulses from his brain. According to the Center for Bionic Medicine at the Northwestern Feinberg School of Medicine, he now just thinks "close hand" and his artificial hand closes.

Our thoughts do not just stay in the mind. They leak into the body. If you are thinking of getting dressed, for example, you are thinking of raising your arm many times. Did you ever notice that when you first wake up in the morning and you are still feeling a bit dopey, thinking of what you are going to wear or what you are going to have for breakfast prepares you for getting out of bed?

Scan Your Mind, Scan Your Body

Thinking can also get us physically tired and stressed. As we think, the mind sends signals to corresponding body parts, and those parts contract slightly. The tension builds up because there may not be a corresponding signal for letting go coming from the brain.

A body scan provides this missing signal. In a relaxation exercise, you learn to relax each muscle one by one and let go of "doing" thoughts. Our thoughts create tension in the body continuously, and not just once a day or once a week. The brain is saying, "do, do, do," all day long. It is not saying, "relax, relax, relax." If you do a body scan once a week, you catch the muscular tension that results from thinking while you do the body scan. For a brief while you taste what relaxation really feels like. But when the exercise is over and you go back from the observing to the thinking mode, the tensions start to come back again.

Three-Breath Relaxation

This book contains fifteen practices (one for every chapter) for cultivating a relaxed attitude. You can find other relaxation exercises such as
body scans online—you can also encounter them in yoga classes. Keep in
mind, however, that the ultimate purpose of these exercises is to make
the relaxation response a natural part of your day. Body scans and yoga
classes can make you familiar with the feel of relaxation so that you can
learn to recognize it. But tension can sneak back on you within minutes
after a relaxation exercise.

Here's the good news, though: once you become familiar with what the
relaxation response feels like, you can evoke it with just three breaths.
Many meditators enjoy doing that with a mindfulness bell that rings at regular intervals. There are a number of such bells online for your computer; I
enjoy the small bell sounds at www.fungie.info/bell and at www.mindful
nessdc.org/bell.

For a *gentle* reminder, set the volume at a low level.

Mindfulness: A Way of Life

Our brain is going to offer us unsolicited thoughts and advice. It is going
to interpret each event. It is going to pass judgment on people and situations all day long. You may be one of the lucky people for whom all these

judgments and advice are positive. If so, you can be thankful that many things in your life will go smoothly and with less stress. But unconditional optimism also has its drawbacks: people lose their shirt as well as make their fortune at the gaming table or in the stock market. The typical new business is no longer in operation five years after being founded. The feeling of certainty is a mental state like any other. We can be "certain" of positive as well as negative outcomes. Mindfulness practice puts a bit of space between our observer stance and *all* kinds of automatic thoughts and mental states so that we gain the freedom of choice. We may still *think* automatically, but we do not have to *act* automatically.

Reuniting Body and Mind

There is more to the mindfulness mantra Be Here Now than meets the eye at first glance. Our body is already here, no doubt about that. This mantra is addressed to the mind, because it is the mind that can slip its moorings and wander away. We understand that intuitively because we have all had the experience. Mindfulness of the breath is a way of anchoring the mind to the body so that the two can stay united.

Some people who encounter mindfulness meditation for the first time fail to appreciate the importance of concentrating on the breath. When the mind and the body separate and start doing different things, it creates problems. In *Buddha's Book of Sleep*, I mention that one of these problems surfaces at bedtime. Consider the scenario where you are in a warm, comfortable bed but your mind is shooting the rapids in an inflatable rubber raft. The excitement of the adventure does not stay only in the mind but leaks into the body. If you were to do a body scan at that moment, you might discover that some of your muscles are tight. If you were aware of your breathing, you might also discover that your breath is not the slow, relaxed breath of a person who is about to doze off, but is uneven. Despite the fact that all the physical conditions for sleeping are there, you may not be able to go to sleep anytime soon.

Are Your Body and Mind at Cross-Purposes?

Another problem with doing one thing while thinking of another is that the body is really doing two things at the same time: it is trying to respond to the situation at hand, while also responding to the demands your thoughts are creating. The two might be at cross-purposes, like attempting to go right and left at the same time. What do you think the result will be when this happens? Right, left, or something else?

I go to the gym at lunchtime. The TV is always on, and there are lots of insurance ads at that time. One ad I often see features a woman falling down the stairs. The implication is that the home is a dangerous place. The problem is never her habit of thinking of other things while going down the stairs. Lack of mindfulness may be hard to prove on an insurance claim, but a remarkable new study coming out of Harvard University has found a way to measure how often we daydream. It is 46.9 percent of the time.

Dr. Matthew Killingsworth and other researchers asked 2,200 volunteers to download an app for the iPhone that provides a menu where they could choose what they were doing, whether they were actually thinking about it, and how happy or sad they felt. The volunteers agreed to take calls at random times during the day, some even taking calls while they were having sex! After analyzing 250,000 calls, the Harvard team concluded that these volunteers spent 46.9 percent of their time awake with their minds wandering. No doubt there is a statistical spread, with some of us more mindful and some less. And somewhere beyond the scale are the 4 percent of adults diagnosed with attention deficit disorder who have additional challenges.

According to a National Institute of Mental Health survey, people with this condition have a history of multiple accidents.

Be Careful!

Mothers all over the world might consider replacing that common interjection addressed to their heedless children with something more to the point, such as, BE HERE NOW, or, WALK MINDFULLY! For the real issue is presence. How can you be careful if you are not even mentally there?

Out of the fog of my childhood one memory stands out. I was coming home from school one afternoon, my bag heavy with books and homework and my mind equally loaded, and I walked into a tree. It was a big tree, and I felt its grooved bark as I reached for my bloody lip. I had broken one of my front teeth. I must have done many other mindless things as a child, but I still remember that one. I have a cap on that tooth.

I was "spaced out," "out to lunch," and "absentminded"—all terms we use for not being present.

Heavy Daydreamers Are Also Less Happy

Another conclusion of the Harvard study cited above was that the people who were most distracted from the task at hand were found to be more likely to report feelings of unhappiness. Dr. Killingsworth concluded that: "Mind-wandering is an excellent predictor of people's happiness." While this study does not really answer the question of which came first, the unhappiness or the mind wandering, it is a confirmation of the value of the "Be Here Now" teachings. We often slide away from the present moment on the slippery slope of automatic thoughts, and automatic thoughts contribute to stress in various ways. The following chapters look at some of these ways in more detail.

The Mind Leads, the Body Follows

Picture a dog. The head is in front, the body behind. The head goes first, and the body follows. Be careful which way the mind is leading! If the mind is leading toward hell, the body will follow, even if all its needs are met to perfection and all its whims and fancies are attended to. Successful and well-off people are not immune from depression. To an outside observer, they appear to have no reason for their depression. It is not the rational, purposive aspect of the mind that is leading them into it. Indeed, the purposive mind is likely trying to draw them out of it. It may be seeing a therapist. But automatic thoughts are the challenge.

Mindfulness involves recognizing. When an automatic thought shows up, we can learn to say, "There it goes again just like the advertising break on TV! I'll take a deep breath and just wait it out." The fact is that, like the TV, our mind has a dual nature. The programs we seek out on TV are like our purposive thoughts: they are beneficial in some way, or we see them as such. They inform or entertain us. The publicity comes automatically, whether we want it or not. Think what would happen to you and your quality of life if you took all the advertising seriously and believed every word. You might go bankrupt before the day is out with new appliances, a new car, new insurance, and a new mortgage!

The advertising appears on the same screen, and comes out of the same speakers on the TV set. Yet we know the difference between it and the programs we choose. Our automatic thoughts and our purposive thoughts have the same voice, and appear on the same mind-screen, yet we often fail to distinguish between them. Mindfulness practice can address this failure.

Making Tracks

Henry David Thoreau wrote: "As a single footstep will not make a path on the earth, so a single thought will not make a pathway in the mind. To make a deep physical path, we walk again and again. To make a deep mental path, we must think over and over the kind of thoughts we wish to dominate our lives." When we hand ourselves over to automatic thoughts without awareness, similar thoughts cross the mind repeatedly, and they make tracks. We may be making tracks of stressful thoughts, of fear or anxiety, without knowing it. Thoreau's advice involves thinking purposively: "We must think over and over the kind of thoughts we wish to dominate our lives." If you want positive tracks to form, think positive thoughts intentionally.

A Paradigm Shift

All the literature about paradise and the Garden of Eden has been inspired by the beauty we find here on Earth—this is the only paradise we know. Mindfulness teachings embody a paradigm shift of sorts—we know paradise through our senses. We know it to the extent that we are able to be in our home in the body. It is the mind that can lead us astray in this paradigm. The mind can separate from the body, leave it behind, and go to places of regret and worry. It can leave the glory of nature behind and get lost in envy, jealousy, ill will, and other negative mental states that are dead ends.

By a stroke of irony, the famous sculpture by Auguste Rodin known as *The Thinker* and usually considered to be glorifying thought, was originally based on *The Divine Comedy* of Dante for a portal entitled *The Gates of Hell*.

Mind and body are not separate, they are parts of one entity. The brain is part of the body, and the body is part of the mind. Mindfulness practice seeks to unite body and mind, and to bring them together each moment.

When You Have a Special Challenge

People suffering from depression or anxiety have the same mental habit of often being in their thoughts that we all have. In addition, they have an added challenge: their thoughts are more often negative. They need mindfulness training even more than the rest of us because it is more important for them to learn to challenge their negative thoughts instead of fusing with them. But their training needs to focus on their issues, and it needs to be adapted to their condition. If you are depressed or anxious, mindfulness can help you, but be forewarned: it is very difficult to master this practice and at the same time figure out a way to apply it to your disorder all by yourself. Fortunately, you do not have to do it by yourself. You can look for a mindfulness meditation coach. Specialized mindfulness-based treatment modalities are also available. Two such modalities are ACT (Acceptance and Commitment Therapy) and Mindfulness Based Cognitive Therapy for Depression. Search for practitioners online: you need private sessions where you can discuss your particular concerns and get help.

◆

Labeling Thoughts

A guided meditation exercise: Sit up straight in the meditation posture and read the text slowly to yourself. Then close the book and do as many of the instructions as you remember. If those proverbial fish discussed in this chapter want to develop awareness of water, they would need frequent reminders such as, "This is water I'm swimming in." In this exercise the reminders are about thoughts. By labeling them we make recognition possible.

I start with consciously taking a few slow, deep breaths.

I put all my attention into my breathing.

When I breathe in, the breath goes into an inner space where I lose track of it.

When I breathe out, it goes into the outer space around me and dissolves.

I do not control what the breath does. I am only aware of my breathing muscles.

I do not know what happens to the breath as it dissolves inside me or outside me.

I am only aware of the short journey of the breath in my nostrils and lungs.

The rest is beyond my awareness.

The breath is a piece of the world that I borrow. It refreshes me for a moment.

Then I return it. There is nothing to hold on to until the next breath.

I live from moment to moment.

I cannot take the same breath twice. Each breath is new and fresh,

and each breath happens a bit differently.

When I become aware that I am thinking, I gently say "thinking" to myself,

and let go. Then I go back to watching my breath.

Now I am not breathing consciously anymore, it is happening by itself.

I just watch it happen, like one watches waves on the beach.

Thoughts arise like bubbles, like the bubbles in a wave.

I label them as they are traveling through my mind.

Like the breath, thoughts come and go.

I let go of them, like I let go of each breath. There is nothing to hold on to.

Did thoughts leave a trace?

Did they leave behind any tension or a residue of emotion?

Scanning my body, I check that I am not holding on to any tension anywhere.

I loosen up, and let go.

Thoughts leave behind tension and emotion when I get entangled in them.

Now I am more vigilant: I label them as they arise.

I just say "thinking" as I am aware of a thought.

I stay light and free.

3.

Mindfulness Training

I know of no other single thing so conducive to misery as this
uncultivated, untrained mind.
I know of no other single thing so conducive to well-being as this
cultivated, well-trained mind.

—THE BUDDHA

Which are you, mindful or mindfull? In the first case, you have a spacious mind that is open to new possibilities; in the second case, you have a mind full of opinions, prejudices, and notions.

This distinction has a venerable history going back to the nineteenth century.

Nan-in, who was a Japanese master, received a university professor who came to inquire about Zen.

As Nan-in served him tea, he kept on pouring after the visitor's cup was full, and continued to pour as it overflowed.

When the professor saw that the master was not stopping, he exclaimed, "Stop! The cup is already full, there's no more room."

The master looked up. "You are like this cup, full of your own opinions and speculations. I cannot show you Zen unless you empty your cup first."

I prefer to believe that the master in question was a gracious host, and had already tried to show his guest some Zen and was met with resistance. Perhaps the professor was a familiar visitor and the master already knew whom he was dealing with. In all fairness to professors, you don't have to be one to be a know-it-all—many people who in fact know very little can be quite opinionated and full of their own ideas.

The trouble with "mindfulness" is that it gets in the way of one's ability to be in the moment and open to experience.

I started my own mindfulness practice with these two fundamentals of openness to experience and willingness to be in the moment. And also with awareness of breath, which anchored these two principles firmly in my body.

Then it became clear that remembering was also important: life's many distractions constantly pull us away from the awareness of breath. We have to *remember* to return to that awareness in order to practice being present in a meaningful way.

Soon after, it became clear that "coming to your senses" was an important part of this practice: we tend to be in our thoughts a lot, and thoughts can take us away from the moment. The senses take in the present moment, and coming to our senses grounds us in the body.

Awareness of emotions and other mental states followed. With that also came an understanding of positive and negative mental states and the practice of happiness. Once the gaze is turned inward, it is hard not to notice the dark clouds as well as the sunshine, the storms as well as the blue skies there.

Then the practice of happiness quickly led to a consideration of relationships.

Remember the caterpillar in *Alice in Wonderland*?

It goads Alice toward deepening her sense of self:

"Who are you?" said the Caterpillar.

Alice is spurred to contemplate impermanence and change:

"I know who I was when I got up this morning, but I think I must have been changed several times since then."

Then it urges her to develop emotional awareness:

"Keep your temper," said the Caterpillar.

My encounter with mindfulness has had a similar effect on me, provoking me toward greater awareness on many different fronts. Indeed, the scope of mindfulness is wide-reaching. If you encountered it while studying and practicing Buddhism, then it is a part of Buddhist practice for you. If you encountered it as part of a Mindfulness Based Stress Reduction course, then it is a way of reducing stress. If you encountered it during the course of Mindfulness Based Cognitive Therapy, then it is part of a counseling modality. Mindfulness is all of these and more.

In a *New York Times* article, Gina Kolata tells the story of how mindful swimming helped one athlete get to the top of the pack. She writes that: "Like many distance swimmers who spend endless hours in the pool,

Natalie Coughlin, 30, used to daydream as she swam laps. She'd been a competitive swimmer for almost her entire life, and this was the way she—and many others—managed the boredom of practice."

But at one point Coughlin realized that swimming while daydreaming only allowed her to get in the miles—it did not allow her to reach her full potential. So she started to concentrate on what she was doing, she stayed focused on her technique during the practice.

"That's when I really started improving," she said. "The more I did it, the more success I had."

Ms. Coughlin won five medals in the 2008 Beijing Olympics, including a gold medal.

Natalie Coughlin's mindfulness practice had a very narrow focus—swimming. In contrast, learning to live with less stress necessitates a wider focus, because stress reaches into every area of life. A more general approach to mindfulness training is needed.

Many people start this training with enthusiasm. Then they come face-to-face with themselves. Sometimes this is not a pleasant experience:

"How do I stop ruminating?"

"How do I stop anxious thoughts?"

"How do I deal with negative thoughts?"

These are common questions during the first weeks of my twelve-week course. Meditation teachers from Buddha on have faced them and developed training strategies to tame the mind, reduce stress, and increase well-being. My method is a little different from Buddha's—it does not involve becoming a monk. It does require regular practice, however, prefera-bly every day. For one's own practice will eventually answer these questions.

At the beginning, mindfulness comes and goes. It may be present for brief moments when we are reminded of it, but then absent for a long time. The purpose of mindfulness practice is to lengthen these brief moments of mindfulness, and shorten the long periods of "mindlessness" between them. States of mind are like habits in a way: like habits, they are a form of shorthand. In anxiety, for example, we have a set reaction of fearfulness that fits all circumstances. We do not have to bother reasoning out each situation rationally—we have a "one size fits all" reaction, and we carry it around with us. This feels so natural that we may not even be aware of how and where it comes from. It just happens. The Buddha said that the first step in transforming suffering is awareness. We need to be aware that we are continually producing anxious thoughts, or sad thoughts, or angry thoughts, before we can start the process of change.

Regular practice is necessary because consciously accepting the neces-sary attitude changes is not enough. Our attitudes and patterns of thinking and reacting have become automatic—they have become habits. We have been practicing them for a lifetime. Just making resolutions for change does not even make a dent. Resolutions are soon forgotten—often as soon as the class is over for the evening. We need to develop new and more whole-some habits. Habits have staying power, but they also take time to form.

We have *all* spent years learning new habits, but few of us remember the experience. We all learned to speak. We all learned to walk. We learned to read and write. Learning the habit of mindfulness is no different. But is it worth it? That is a decision each person has to make for herself. If your old attitudes are making you too stressed for your liking or for your good health, you might like to make a change. Reading this book will help you decide, but that decision is all yours.

Interesting fact: many of us have had the experience of learning new skills since childhood as well—we know it can be done. We have all learned to drive. Remember what it was like when you had no automatic driving reactions and you had to think of each move consciously? Thirty-two percent of teenagers can text blindfolded. Many others learn to play musical instruments in high school, and people of all ages learn to play golf or tennis. Most Swiss, Quebecois, Scandinavians, and Dutch can speak a second language. All of these skills involve painstakingly learning new habits. They involve training our inner elephant to do tricks on demand.

We do not have to practice for months or years before we start to reap the benefits of mindfulness. When we were learning to walk, there was a payoff right at the beginning: we managed to walk from Daddy to Mommy and got a big hug. Mindfulness practice is also like that—there are payoffs in the form of small reductions in stress with each stage of the practice.

Attitude change is one of the big issues in mindfulness training. In the beginning, we first train the elephant trainer, the conscious mind. We must first accept consciously that mindfulness is beneficial, and that we want it to be a part of our life. During this phase, we may do some reading and attend talks and retreats. If we stop there, the conscious and the unconscious mind may pull in different directions, because now they have different values. The conscious mind has embraced a less judgmental and more relaxed attitude, but has not yet passed this attitude on to the deeper levels of the mind where habits and attitudes reside. The bigger part of mindfulness training starts at this point: the training of the unconscious mind. Now the elephant trainer is ready to train the elephant. Will she take the trouble to do it?

A Zen Koan

In a Zen koan, two Zen masters are chatting.

One asks how the bodhisattva Quan Yin (also called Avalokiteshvara) uses her many hands. The question is a good one because Quan Yin, the bodhisattva of compassion, is said to have a thousand arms and hands. She has dedicated her life to working unceasingly for the enlightenment and the benefit of all beings. If you have young children, aging parents, and a job, perhaps you have longed to have more than just two arms sometimes. But how does Quan Yin use those thousand arms and hands when we have enough trouble using just one pair?

"It's just like a person in the middle of the night reaching back in search of a pillow," comes the answer. In other words, she does it automatically. It has become second nature to her—she does not have to think about it. She has trained her elephant and programmed her unconscious.

Compare this with a story Richard once told me. Richard was one of my t'ai chi teachers. In addition to his very intensive t'ai chi practice, he studied aikido and kung fu. He lived and breathed martial arts. He used to say that if he saw two guys walking toward him in the park, he had already figured out what he would do in case they decided to attack him. One night in the middle of his sleep, Richard sensed a slight commotion. He woke up to find that he already had his partner in a choke hold. The commotion he felt was his partner innocently turning around in her sleep. Richard had acted automatically because he had also programmed his unconscious through years of intensive practice, but in a different direction.

We are always programming our unconscious, though we may not realize it. We are programming it or reinforcing its previous programming every time we react with fear and stress, and every time we do things half-heartedly.

Elephant Training

Our consciousness is like the beam of a flashlight in the night—it illuminates whatever we are pointing it at. It can illuminate different objects and areas, but only one at a time. The rest remains in the dark. When we attend to something, much more remains in darkness than is illuminated, just like what happens with a flashlight. If we want the dark areas in our minds to vibrate in harmony with our values, we need to train the whole mind.

The Buddha used training a wild elephant as a metaphor for training the mind.

Training Real Elephants

It may look like the rider, our conscious mind, is no match for the elephant—that big bundle of habits, unconscious impulses, genetic dispositions, likes, and dislikes that we all have. The sheer difference in size of available resources suggests this. In the *Dhammapada*, however, Buddha affirms that it is possible:

"My mind used formerly to go off wandering wherever it felt like, following its own inclination, but today I shall control it carefully, like a mahout does a rutting elephant."

Not only the Buddha, but also the many non-metaphorical elephant trainers I met at the Elephant Camp in Chiang Mai, Thailand, had succeeded in this tricky undertaking. Their real elephants played darts, they played football, gave massages (to those who had the nerve to lie still under the huge beast), they played harmonicas and painted lovely pictures of flowers. Afterward they gave you adorable embraces with their trunks and posed for pictures. Then they waved their trunks in your face until you came up with a tip that they carefully picked up and handed over to their trainers. Those trainers had also succeeded in establishing a harmonious kind of control and intimacy with their erstwhile wild elephants. It is doable.

Untrained Horses

I do not want us to get sidetracked by the exoticism of elephants. Elephants were a common sight in India in Buddha's day and not at all exotic. One Buddhist sutra describes King Ajatasattu paying Buddha a visit with his retinue mounted on five hundred elephants. I have difficulty visualizing the scene—perhaps you have a better imagination than I. It was a different world. It may be easier to talk about horse training with the same import.

The first time I rode a horse, it felt like lying down and scratching its back on the grass—with me still in the saddle! Another time we were passing by a lake and my horse decided to cool itself down by going in, ignoring all my attempts to prevent it from doing so. Soon I was in the lake up to my buttocks. The worst was when I went up a mountain path with a friend. On the way up, we had the impression that the horses were doing our bidding—they turned in all the right directions as we pulled on the reins. Actually the horses were following a well-worn routine up that hill. They completely ignored us on the way down—they galloped downhill at full speed to get to the barn for water and hay. I managed to hang on, but my friend fell face-first on the gravel road. She was a schoolteacher starting work the next day. She had to meet her new students with her face completely bandaged, with only eyes showing. Fortunately her scratches and black-and-blue spots eventually healed without leaving a trace.

Such incidents also happen as a result of our "inner horse" taking control. They are called hangovers, eating binges, and sexual misconduct. Indeed, Thich Nhat Hanh is fond of recounting a Zen story about a rider who is galloping along. A friend sees him passing by and shouts, "Where are you going?" The man shouts back, "I don't know, ask the horse."

Thich Nhat Hanh likens the horse in this story to our habit energy. Notice that the horses in my life were also following their habits—the habit of lying in the grass to scratch, the habit of going in the lake to cool down on a hot day, and the habit of galloping toward the barn to satisfy their hunger or thirst.

Horsemanship

If your only experience of horsemanship is limited to reading about my adventures, you may well come to the conclusion that training a horse is impossible. That would be a pity. The fact that you and I have no clue about how to train a horse does not mean that it can't be done. The book *The Horse Whisperer* shows in an imaginative and compassionate way how even a deeply scarred animal can recover through proper training.

The metaphoric horse shares the same body with the rider. No one else can train her without the rider's permission and cooperation. The rider is the only one who can speak to her inner horse directly. Others have to go through the intermediary of the rider because the horse and the rider are in fact different aspects of the same person.

Mindfulness Training in Prison

Like everyone else, you and I may have certain challenges that cause stress in our lives. But our issues pale in comparison to those of convicts in a maximum-security prison, many of whom have committed brutal crimes such as murder. Their inner horses and elephants are truly wild and untamed. Could mindfulness training work with such a population?

Kiran Bedi decided to find out. She had just been appointed inspector general of Indian prisons in 1993, and she was inspired by the successful example of a Vipassana program (a form of intensive mindfulness training) in another Indian prison that had taken place some twenty years earlier. Her experiment became a huge success—over one thousand inmates took the Vipassana offering in a large, crowded, maximum-security prison. The transformation of the inmates at the end of the course is palpable in the movie that was made of the event. *Doing Time, Doing Vipassana* won the prestigious Golden Spire Award at the 1998 San Francisco International Film Festival among 1,600 entries from fifty-eight countries. In announcing the award, the festival management added:

"The jury was moved by this insightful and poignant exposition on Vipassana. The teaching of this meditation as a transformation device has many implications for people everywhere, providing the cultural, social, and political institutions can embrace and support its liberating possibility."

If you want inspiration and hope as you contemplate mindfulness training, please watch that movie. It has inspired the King County North Rehabilition Facility in Seattle, Washington, to offer Vipassana courses to its inmates, and to study the effects of the course in reducing recidivism. It found that only half of the inmates who took the ten-day retreat were incarcerated again, compared to 75 percent of the general prison population.

Daily Meditation

An intensive retreat in the Vipassana or Zen tradition can mean ten-plus hours of sitting every day. For many beginners it is difficult to go from zero meditation to ten hours a day. Daily meditation for shorter periods is a gentler way to get started. I enjoy my daily sittings—the day's experiences nourish my meditation and the meditation enriches my daily life.

But beware of meditating with a purpose. We are used to doing things with a purpose—we do not prepare a meal just to prepare a meal. But even though we may have a motive—such as stress reduction—in mind as we start meditation practice, we must learn to keep that motive on the back burner. Purpose is achieved differently and more indirectly in meditation. Whether it is creativity or stress reduction, the way toward a meditation goal is not necessarily direct. In fact, goals and strivings can get in the way of meditation. Meditation is about the journey, not the destination—its focus is on being, not on doing.

Meditation Coaching

Meditation was never meant to be practiced without guidance. The Buddha gave many talks about practice. His instructions have survived, and enable us to reconstruct his teaching. Many of them were uttered within a context, in response to a question or a problem. Imagine what would happen if the responses of a modern-day psychotherapist were studied without the questions or the problems that gave rise to them!

In Thich Nhat Hanh's retreats, a group-sharing period of about ninety minutes led by a teacher is scheduled into every day. In Zen retreats, several private interviews with the teacher, called dokusan, punctuate the day. Such private or semiprivate interactions with a teacher are an essential part of meditation practice, because meditation involves changing our habitual mental patterns. Without personal instruction and feedback, an anxious person might just sit for a whole meditation period and worry!

If you are contemplating joining a meditation group or going to a retreat, consider this issue. Inquire if opportunities for private or semiprivate time with an instructor are offered. If they are voluntary, take advantage of them.

Doing Things Wholeheartedly Is a Kind of Meditation

Our unconscious mind is a whiz at multitasking. Right now, mine is digesting my supper, beating my heart, adjusting my blood pressure and body temperature, and finding letters on the computer keyboard as I think of words. It can do all that simultaneously because that is its nature and it has ample resources at its disposal. The conscious mind can only do one thing at a time. It deals with this limitation by outsourcing, by unloading as many activities as it can onto the unconscious mind. The result is that we often drive, wash dishes, and chop vegetables on autopilot. Perhaps the evolutionary reason was that then the conscious mind would be free to focus on more vital and important tasks, such as figuring out where its next meal would come from or spotting an interesting sexual partner. But that was a few million years ago. Today this same tendency just creates a disconnect between mind and body, the body doing things without awareness while the mind thinks of other things. To reverse this tendency, just sit and get in touch with your breath. It is not difficult to do.

You can get a meditation bench or cushion and set up a special spot, or you can meditate where you are:

- in bed before you get up (just prop the pillows under your buttocks and sit),

- in the kitchen while the rice is cooking,

- or in the living room or the backyard when there is a quiet moment.

◆

Letting Go and Being Present

Our autonomic nervous system (ANS) responds to challenges in the environment by raising our blood pressure and our heart rate, and by making other adjustments. The sympathetic and parasympathetic divisions of the ANS usually function in complementary fashion, the sympathetic division preparing the body for the fight-or-flight response, and the parasympathetic division acting as the rest and digest system.

As we get ready to jump over a puddle, the body gets ready for the effort automatically. But once the jump is over, does it go back to a relaxed state by itself?

Our day can be like a long street full of puddles, from the morning routine of getting kids ready for school to fighting traffic to get to work, to the curveballs we encounter at work. For many of us, the stress just keeps mounting. The sympathetic system does its job well to get the body to rise up to the tests and trials we face, but the parasympathetic system does not always get a chance to kick in and establish the balance by bringing our metabolism back to a normal, resting state.

Mindfulness and Balance

Our propensity for being in our thoughts rather than in the moment can get in the way of letting go and returning to a baseline of relaxed functioning. For when the actual stressful moment passes, the memory of it remains. Thoughts such as, "Wow, I almost had an accident," and emotional reactions of anger or irritation keep the stress reaction going. Between brooding over past narrow escapes and worrying about future ones, the parasympathetic system does not always get a chance to return the organism to a resting state. There is no actual challenge between the puddles on the road, only memory and anticipation. But if we are not in the moment, we do not benefit from a lull in environmental stressors. To benefit from them, we need to be in the moment, and present to the actual circumstances. We need to "get our mind off it." And we need to avoid "getting all worked up" over nothing. We do not have to respond emotionally to every routine situation.

Read the instructions slowly, then sit and practice what you remember. You may remember different things each time—thus, your sitting may have a different flavor each time you do this exercise. If, in the course of your sitting, you find that your meditation is not going satisfactorily, come back to the text and read the instructions again.

I take a few slow and deep breaths,

relaxing my muscles with each breath.

I let go of tension in my face muscles, hands,

shoulders, abdomen, legs, and feet as I breathe.

Only the postural muscles in my back

and other muscles responsible for my balance and posture are engaged.

I breathe in fresh air that relaxes and nourishes every cell.

I breathe out tension.

I check in with my mind,

and let go of any lingering thoughts and concerns.

Thoughts come. And sometimes they go, and sometimes they stay.

Now I make sure that they go as I breathe out.

I clear my mind with each breath.

I empty my mind as I breathe out.

I make sure that the thoughts that come also go.

Thoughts and feelings come automatically.

But they do not always go away by themselves.

Clearing my mind with each breath, I stay in the moment.

With each breath, I let go of any lingering thoughts or concerns.

I am available and present for what happens *now*.

BREATHING is happening now.

Slow and rhythmic breathing like waves rolling over the sand on a beach.

I am like a beach.

Waves of breath come and go.

Freshening my body and mind.

I sit, enjoying the waves of breath

as they roll in and out.

With each breath I scan my body and mind

and let go of any tension I find.

Thoughts are welcome.

They can stay for one breath.

Then, with a smile, I clear them out.

With each breath, I am consciously clearing my body of tension

and my mind of thoughts.

I am fresh and free for this breath,

and for this moment.

4.

Inspiration

We meditate to discover our own identity, our right place in the universe.
Through meditation, we acquire, and eventually acknowledge our
connection to an inner power source that has the ability to
transform our outer world.

—JULIA CAMERON

June was talking about her difficulty getting into creative writing: "I know where I am, and I know where I want to go. But it is as if there is a chasm between the two. A chasm full of mud, the mud of my own lack of confidence and insecurity. I fear that I'm not good enough, and I do not know how to bridge that gap." As she talked, her hands were giving me a visual picture of the gap.

I wasn't sure that she had the right picture of creativity in her mind. The "mud" she spoke about is the raw material of our life. Good writers have not built bridges over it; instead they have refined the raw material into gold. "No mud, no lotus," says Thich Nhat Hanh. "Lotus flowers do not grow on marble."

I also felt that June was blocked because she saw creativity as the work of her conscious mind. The conscious mind is only a small part of the mind. Even if one were able to come up with something using only that small part, it may feel dry and contrived instead of spontaneous and truly creative. The juicy stuff comes when we are connected to the unconscious.

In the last chapter I emphasized the importance of purposive thinking at the expense of automatic thoughts. My main purpose in doing this is to develop awareness so that we learn to recognize which is which. I do not want to give the impression that spontaneous thoughts are "bad," and purposive thoughts are "good." Spontaneous thoughts can create stress when they are driven by habit, or by negative emotions like fear, anger, and anxiety. But they can also represent flashes of inspiration and insight. Learning to recognize the difference is important if we want to lead an inspired life.

The function of the conscious mind is to organize, direct, and put to work the unconscious. Later it can switch to evaluating and editing what the unconscious mind comes up with. Functioning as an executive is what the conscious mind is good at. And just as some executives are better at tapping into the talent at their disposal, our conscious mind can be good or lousy at that task. It depends on our attitude toward the unconscious, and our relationship with it. Meditation improves this relationship. Our ability to tap into the unconscious can improve with time as the unconscious ceases to be a total mystery—the land of the unknown. It will always remain a little mysterious, but we gradually develop a sense of familiarity with its mystery and a working relationship with it.

Conscious Mind as the Interface

Inspiration does not always come out of the blue. Often it comes in response to a question. The question can be either conscious or unconscious. It can be something that has been on your mind for years, or something recent that you just cannot figure out. I think of my conscious mind as the interface that enables me to connect with the rest of my mind. There is more to the mind than meets the eye, just like there is more to your computer than the interface with which you interact. Its inner workings are not intelligible to most of us. The user-friendliness of the computer screen makes the whole thing appear deceptively simple. Even when we learn a complex program, we are only learning about its interface.

The human brain has been described as the most complex thing in the entire universe. It is much more complex than a computer. It has roots in the body, roots in our evolutionary past, and roots in the present. Yet the relative simplicity of its interface—our consciousness—also makes it appear deceptively simple.

Ask a Question

One way to engage the unconscious mind is by asking questions.

Zen koans are questions. They turn the conscious mind into the questioner. The kinds of questions used in koan practice are not ones that can be solved by research or by Googling them. Indeed, I just tried Googling my first koan, "Who is listening?" as an experiment, and got totally off-the-wall answers like, "When the Pope speaks Latin, who is listening?"

That question "Who is listening?" was on my mind constantly as I meditated in the Diamond Zendo in Honolulu twenty-five years ago. In those days, the Diamond Zendo was at the edge of the forest, and the birdsongs at dawn were exquisite. "Who is listening?" Aitken Roshi would ask me several times each day in private interviews, and my conscious mind would make up "reasonable" answers that were rejected—until I gave up fabricating answers and learned to just sit and pay attention.

After I went through this process of questioning as part of my Zen practice and noticed the birth of an answer, I got hooked. I decided to use the process more often. Indeed, my current attitude is, "Any time spent *without* a burning question is time wasted." Thus, right now I will continue to write until I no longer know what to say. Then "What comes next?" will be my koan for the next little while. It is like turning a problem over to a research team. This particular team has all my life experience at its disposal—my whole life since I was a baby, all the books I read, the movies I saw, and all the conversations I participated in are there somewhere in my unconscious. The problem is that this resource is not alphabetized! My conscious attempts at accessing it draw blanks. The unconscious mind has some kind of a random-access algorithm that works. I do not have direct control over this process—it is organic, like plants growing, and like growing plants it can also take its sweet time. But now I have learned not to throw up my hands in despair and say, "I give up. I don't know how to continue." I just wait.

This has its rewards as well as its frustrations.

The reward is that when a continuation or an answer comes from the whole mind, it rings true.

By the way, *who* is listening?

Just listening.

Better to focus on the experience rather than make up stories about the listener or metaphysical speculations about her.

Dreams

Just like our automatic thoughts, a dream can be an inconsequential rehashing of the day's events or a source of important insights.

The unconscious mind works in pictures and stories. However, its point of view can be quite different from the way the conscious mind sees things. Our desires and aversions often skew our conscious understanding. The unconscious mind has a different point of view. Sometimes its point of view is wiser, because it doesn't wear the same blinders. For the same reason, what it comes up with can be hard to understand or interpret. Poems and Zen stories have this directness of expression. Academic writing does not.

When I went on a retreat with Robert Aitken Roshi twenty-five years ago, he was always exhorting me to be more direct and intimate and less discursive. I'm still working on that.

I found an echo of Robert Aitken's charge in the Leonard Cohen interview with Paul Zollo. There, Cohen makes the surprising statement:

"I haven't had an idea in a long, long time. And I'm not sure I ever had one."
He explains himself a little later: "When I say that I don't have any ideas, it
doesn't come to me in the form of an idea. It comes in the form of an image."
In other words, not discursive, but direct and concrete. And more "Zen."

Meditating

Meditation can pry open the door to inspiration: instead of just waiting
for it to arrive in its own sweet time, we can coax it out by meditating. A
daily meditation period is a period of intimacy with oneself. In Thich Nhat
Hanh's words, "Meditation is offering your genuine presence to yourself in
every moment." I did quite a bit of "research" for this book on the meditation cushion.

Use the Brain, or Be Used by It

The brain tells us to worry, to regret, to eat more ice cream, and to drink
more beer. It daydreams and imagines pleasant outcomes. Or it imagines
worst-case scenarios. All this output just happens. And usually we sit and
take it all in, dutifully listening and believing it all to be true.

But we can also put this powerhouse to work in order to serve our aspi-
rations, our values, and our purposes.

Inspiration can come spontaneously, just like automatic thoughts. Also like them, it does not carry a banner, nor is it announced by fanfare. Nevertheless, it needs to be recognized and honored, even though it may come uninvited. We need to be open and ready for its grace when and if it arrives.

How do we recognize inspiration?

Koan training in the Zen tradition is training in recognizing inspiration and insight. The student brings all kinds of answers to a koan during interviews, answers she makes up, answers coming from superficial thoughts and ideas. The teacher's task is to separate the wheat from the chaff. As her superficial ideas get rejected, the student slowly learns what is *not* inspiration. Then, when she stumbles on an insight and it gets recognized, she sees the difference. As this scenario gets repeated many times, she gains more experience in recognizing the real thing. A student geologist digging for gold encounters much dirt, rocks, and "fool's gold" before she learns to recognize the real stuff.

Dharma talks are another source of training in recognizing inspiration. In a Dharma talk, the teacher presents her own inspiration. Dharma talks can sometimes appear puzzling for that reason. Thich Nhat Hanh often exhorts his audience to let his talks soak "like Dharma rain" into the ground of the mind. This is listening with an open mind—a different kind of activity from listening to the vacuum cleaner salesman's pitch.

Henry David Thoreau found inspiration while walking in nature. He went walking four hours a day carrying a notebook. He did not want to miss any inspired ideas that came to him during his walks. Inspiration needs to be written down when it shows up. Suddenly, the door is flung open and insights appear. That is a precious moment, not to be missed. If we do not record it, it will fade away like a dream. Short-term memory will not hold it.

To paraphrase Thomas Edison, "Creative work is one percent inspiration, ninety-nine percent perspiration." I feel, however, that the perspiration Edison speaks of is also inspired perspiration. It smells sweet. A flash of inspiration may provide the grand idea for a work—in this case, it provided the title and the general idea for the book I am writing. But the ideas for each chapter, and indeed, for each paragraph, also contain some inspiration. That one percent Thomas Edison talks about is a little bit like the one percent of salt on the plate: it is a small part of the meal, but without it every mouthful would be quite tasteless.

Let's say that you are working on a poem, and the part of your brain that deals with language is hard at work on it. You are stuck on a word that does not seem to exist. You have already tried all the obvious choices that came to you, including some from the dictionary. None of them seem right. You feel blocked. So you stop and do something else, perhaps prepare lunch or go for a walk. But a poem is more than language. While you were taking a break, the question spread out to different areas of the brain, and something like a group of people brainstorming happened, except that in this case it was the different brain areas that were brainstorming with each other. Now, when you come back to the poem, you see it differently. You were stuck on a word, but now images and ideas are helping you move forward. You see that you do not have to use that particular metaphor or turn of phrase. There is a better way to say it, and it does not need that word that is missing from the dictionary. That idea ostensibly came "out of the blue." We say that because we do not see how it happened. But I think that it involved the whole brain, or a larger part of it than when we were stuck. We are not dealing only with words anymore. I will venture to say that inspiration comes from an enlarged perspective, and that is what makes it precious.

I feel that purposive thinking is what Edison means by "perspiration." Sometimes this is just what is needed: a legal opinion or a plumbing problem may require only a limited set of references. But when none of the tools and wrenches in the plumber's truck solve the problem, a creative approach may be necessary. That is when inspiration is priceless. If you need a creative approach to redesigning your bathroom, you may need an inspired plumber.

Inspiration can move us beyond the impossible. When purposive thinking is leavened with inspiration, the brain is using all its power. Without a touch of creativity, we may be just rehashing old scenarios and taking the same dead-end streets over and over. We may be stuck. This can be stressful.

I think it is the "impossible" that prepares the ground for inspiration. If there is no problem, no creative solution is necessary. When we see things this way, we are more willing to tackle problems that seem to have no obvious solutions.

Positive Feelings Foster Creativity

What qualities make a person creative?

If you take an informal poll, you will probably find that most people associate creativity with intelligence, accomplishment, or even "genius." Not many of us intuitively consider "feeling good" as an important ingredient of creativity. Yet in summarizing her own and other researchers' findings, Barbara Fredrickson concludes that positive feelings play an important role in creativity.

In her book *Positivity*, she writes: "Positivity opens us. The first core truth about positive emotions is that they open our hearts and minds, making us more receptive and more creative." When we are stimulated by positive feelings such as joy, gratitude, serenity, interest, hope, pride, amusement, inspiration, awe, and love—Fredrickson's list of the principal positive emotions—we see more possibilities. Surprisingly, this even applies to visual perception—we see more detail and background in a picture when we are feeling good. Additionally, physicians make faster and more accurate diagnoses, students do better on tests, and managers make more effective decisions. This is because "positivity broadens your outlook, bringing more possibilities into view."

Even more important for the subject of this book, Fredrickson found that positivity improved the ability of university students to handle stress.

◆

Listening to Sensations

When we want to de-stress and do not succeed, "the body is not listening to the mind" may be the perceived problem. But the real problem is the other way around: the mind is not listening to the body. It is listening to its thoughts about the body. The essence of this meditation is to stay with the sensations and not slip into the thinking mode. The challenge is that when there is no strong sensation, the body speaks very quietly.

Raising the buttocks by sitting on a firm meditation cushion is the key to having a straight back. You can search for one online. Another alternative is a meditation bench. However, don't let the lack of these meditation supplies deter you from meditating: you can just sit up straight in a chair or on some folded blankets.

I am aware of the sensations of breathing.

I bring my awareness from my thoughts to my sensations.

As I breathe in, there is a little coolness around my nostrils.

I feel my abdomen rising and falling,

and my belt or clothes readjust themselves.

Sensations are different from thoughts.

With sensations, there are no words.

I pay attention to the quality and the feel of the sensations of breathing.

I focus on the sensations themselves as I breathe.

This is different from thinking about my breathing.

My body speaks in sensations.

It does not speak in words.

I bring my attention to other sensations:

When I hear sounds, I notice the quality and the feel of sounds.

I experience sound as sound,

I do not experience it as words such as bell, car, or airplane.

I listen with my ears

and not with my mind.

Now I bring my attention to the sensations of sitting.

I tune in to the sensations from my feet and legs.

What do sensations feel like?

When I attach words to sensations,

words such as discomfort or tension, my mind reacts to the words.

Now I experience just the quality of the sensations themselves.

I am not thinking about my feet and legs.

I am listening to them. My feet and legs do not speak English.

Next I tune in to the sensations in my arms and hands.

Do both my hands feel exactly the same?

Now I tune in to my face muscles.

Sometimes I experience worry as tension in my forehead or eyebrows.

Now my forehead and eyebrows are relaxed.

Sometimes I experience stress as tension in my neck and shoulders.

There is no stress now.

There is nothing to do, and nowhere to go now.

No obligations. I can relax in contentment.

I breathe in contentment, I breathe out contentment.

I feel contentment in my body, and also in my mind.

Contentment is an open kind of feeling, open and expanding.

If I can be content for one breath, maybe I can be content a little longer.

Maybe I can stay content for a whole minute.

I sit enjoying my breath, enjoying the feel of my body,

and basking in contentment.

I notice that my mind is quiet now.

Breathing in, breathing out, I notice how light the air is.

I stay with the quality of lightness,

I feel light in body and spirit, like the air I breathe.

◆

PART TWO

Control and Acceptance

5.

Control

One ship drives east and another drives west by the same winds
that blow. It's the set of the sails and not the gales that
determines the way they go.
—ELLA WHEELER WILCOX

If you are a sailor, you are quite aware that you do not control the wind. A regatta is quite a different kind of event from a car race. Race car drivers control the accelerator pedal. Sailors don't. All the sailboats in a race are powered by the same wind. Yet one of them manages to go faster than others and wins the race. How? To the uninitiated it is mystifying. The skill of a sailor is invisible to the rest of us. But it is there, a masterful mix of acceptance and control.

A sailor who does not accept the prevailing wind conditions would have a difficult time. She is in the wrong business. Sailing is a better metaphor than, say, driving for living a successful and productive life. Drivers want more control over their lives—they don't even want to accept road conditions such as speed limits and stop signs. They feel they are in charge. They do not expect to suddenly run out of gas like a sailor runs out of wind when it stalls. And when the driving is slow, as in a traffic jam, drivers fret, thinking that this is not the way it is supposed to be. They see the traffic jam as a sort of error: it happened because something went wrong somewhere.

A sailor learns to develop a more accepting attitude toward the wind.

A participant in one of my groups told us that this is not entirely true. He occasionally sails, and knows of sailors who do get impatient when the wind falls. My reply was that those weekend sailors still do more driving than sailing, and their primary metaphor in life remains driving. They expect to be "in the driver's seat" even when they hop into their boats—they keep the same mind-set.

Farming is another one of these activities where humans are in partnership with nature. A farmer can do everything right, but too much rain or lack of it, soil conditions, and pests can still wreak havoc with his harvest. Again, a mix of acceptance and control is required.

Man Proposes, God Disposes

Some time ago, in love with the poetry of Rumi and Hafiz, I decided to take a closer look at Sufism—the spiritual path that nourished these poets. Together with an abundance of gorgeous poetry, I discovered a deeply religious outlook in which success and failure in any enterprise were ascribed mostly to the will of an omniscient and inscrutable God. He determines the outcome of our efforts. The interjection "Insha'Allah" (God willing) is part of every plan, every proposal in the world of the Sufis.

In contrast, the brash confidence of our time has gone to the opposite extreme. Lack of rain? No problem. Just divert a couple of rivers. Pests? No problem. Just spray some very toxic stuff and kill them. Soil conditions? We can genetically engineer seeds to grow in poor soil, or add some chemicals to alter the soil composition. No need for "Insha'Allah." "Yes, we can," as President Obama used to say. He doesn't say that much during his second term. Political reality has caught up with him.

Ecological reality is catching up with modern farmers as well. Our control over nature has been vastly expanded, but its limits are also becoming obvious. Expecting every problem to be solved, every inconvenience eliminated creates extra stress, as we are now more apt to ascribe our setbacks to some kind of error or personal failure.

We all need a spiritual path to regain a sense of balance in our lives.

That balance is between our illusion of total control and the reality of the limits of our control. Conflict between these two brings stress. We rant and rave internally, and sometimes externally about things that we cannot control. We have trouble with acceptance.

In Buddhism, the part that we cannot control derives from the interconnectedness of phenomena. Codependent arising, a cornerstone of Buddhist vision, is derived from the interpenetration of phenomena. It means that things happen not only because of our efforts—conditions must also be right. Some of these conditions, as described in the butterfly effect, are way beyond our control, or even our knowledge. You could play all your cards right and invest in the right stocks, but a bank failure on the other side of the globe may create a domino effect and cause you to lose money, even though you cannot pronounce the name of the bank or had no idea that it existed.

The expectation that science and technology can solve every problem wasn't always there. Our agrarian ancestors created the monotheistic religions we still practice, and they lived in a world where they had much less control over their lives. When, during the first session of a class, I asked the participants what had brought them here, one man said that he hoped to cope with chronic pain better. Another participant jokingly suggested Advil. There was no Advil two thousand years ago. Acceptance was the only possible attitude toward pain, and toward other health challenges. Our technological advances today create the illusion that all is under control. When we cannot control pain with drugs, we are often shocked and angry. The dark areas beyond our control have receded, but they are still there. Sickness, old age, and death are still present today, as they were in Buddha's day, but our acceptance of them has diminished.

A gardener is like the sailor and the farmer: she is subject to the sun and the rain. She has no control over them. She has control over many other things having to do with gardening skills, but ultimately her garden can stall just like a sailboat without wind if there is no rain, or too much rain, or rain at the wrong time. The Sufi saying "Man proposes, God disposes" makes a more realistic kind of sense in that setting.

This brings up an interesting diversion: statistics show that men are less stressed than women. This finding puzzles many researchers.

Could it have something to do with the fact that men never have unwanted pregnancies?

Could it be that women have less control over their lives than men do?

I do not have periods, have not experienced PMS or menopause, and have no idea what morning sickness feels like. My breasts never hurt when I run, I have never had to make a personal choice about abortion or worried about breast-feeding recalcitrant babies or about having enough breast milk. With us, the clock continues to tick well into old age. We experience half the rate of childhood sexual abuse, and we suffer much less from conjugal violence.

Women work longer hours—a working mother often has a second shift waiting for her at home after she finishes her day job. Is it any wonder that they are more stressed?

Back to the gender-neutral main subject.

We now expect a solution to every problem, and often we are not disappointed. This reinforces our conviction. The vagaries of nature and of the weather do not faze us much. Today's weekend gardener does not face famine when drought hits. She can still go to the supermarket and stock up her refrigerator. During the historical period when the great monotheistic religions arose, however, this wasn't so, and there was often no alternative to acceptance. Famine in the early spring was a common occurrence in the dark ages.

During the time of Christopher Columbus, many sailors perished at sea. Yet some survived, and even managed to bring our ancestors across the ocean to the New World in those wooden boats powered by puffs of wind.

Faith in God, and humbly accepting His will, had a more practical ring in those days.

Relationships and Control

Apply this awareness of what is in your control and what isn't to matters big and small, and reduce your stress.

Bill, a young man in his late twenties, had joined a group in order to better cope with his feelings of loss over the fact that his longtime girlfriend had decided to break off the relationship. He was flooded with self-doubt and was visibly stressed.

Bill found it helpful to see that what his ex-girlfriend thought or wanted was truly beyond his control, but that he had control over how he reacted to the separation. As the weeks went by, I could see a change—he did not look so distressed anymore. At one session he mentioned that he was skipping an important business meeting to attend that evening's session because he found our group so valuable.

To see what lies in your control is empowering because you hold the cards that matter. In contrast, when you focus on something that is not in your control, you feel helpless because you feel that someone else is calling the shots. Simply put, when you try to control what lies beyond your competence, you are a loser. When you focus on controlling what does lie in your control, you can be a winner. And that makes all the difference in the amount of stress you feel.

◆

The Two Baskets Exercise

A good way of looking at our stress, worries, anxieties, and ruminations is to consider whether we have any control over what we are fretting about. Are we trying to control other people? Are we trying to control events that are clearly beyond our competence?

In the operating room, there is a clear division of responsibility: the anesthesiologist does not reach over the surgeon's elbow to suture a vein, and the surgeon does not go wandering around looking for the instrument she needs. Such a division of labor helps make things go smoothly and skews the odds in favor of the survival of the patient.

Things would also go smoothly in our minds if we were clear about what is our responsibility and what is not. The behavior of other drivers on the road, the behavior of the stock market, and the preferences of our partner are beyond our jurisdiction. Controlling them is not part of our job description in life. We are not responsible for them.

We only have control over our reaction to these and many other events. We have control over our attitude, our behavior, our speech, our goals, and our values. Recognizing the limits of our control is not an exercise in fatalism. We have control over more than we often realize—we do not have to sit and stew in automatic negative thoughts, for example. We can "change the channel," and the direction of our thinking. We can change our eating and drinking habits, how much we exercise . . . the list is long.

Try this exercise:

Put two wastepaper baskets in front of you. Label one IN MY CONTROL and the other OUT OF MY CONTROL, or simply, IN and OUT. Put every thought that occurs to you in one of the baskets. It helps if you actually make the motion of putting something in the basket with your hand. You will find that this is an empowering as well as a limiting exercise. Are you worried about whether your boss will accept the office reorganization proposal you just submitted? Pop it into the OUT basket and let go of it. The outcome is in her hands, not yours. However, you do have control over whether you worry about it or not, so put that worry in the IN basket.

Do a triage for every thought that occurs to you and start filling your IN and OUT baskets. The exercise may prove to have unexpected benefits. For example, the ultimate outcome of a health condition may go in the OUT basket; worrying about it can go in the IN basket. Yet while doing this exercise, you may discover that you have other options besides worrying—more proactive options such as going for a second opinion, or exploring complementary treatments, or taking better care of yourself. Those constructive steps go in the IN basket.

Do you see yourself as a victim? Put that in the IN basket. Victimhood is an interpretation that is in your control. Only the circumstance that triggered "victim" thoughts can go in the OUT basket. Self-pity? Also IN basket.

Some event that triggered your anger? OUT basket.

Your anger? IN basket.

Now start dealing with the contents of the IN basket. You need to deal with every item in that basket if you want to take charge of your life. You can also glance at the OUT basket from time to time to make sure that you are not hanging on to things that are beyond your control. You need to let go of every item in that basket in order to make peace with your world. This is like the Serenity Prayer in action—you accept the things you cannot change, and summon up courage to change the things you can. Hopefully, doing this exercise will create the "wisdom to know the difference" without having to ask for help from divine guidance. You will find that doing this exercise is not that difficult once you start thinking about it rationally; it is a bit like cleaning your desk: Is the item you are looking at useful? Put it in a drawer or in the filing cabinet. Not useful? Toss it.

Useful Worrying

This exercise liberates your mind from automatic worries, which are driven by emotions, and makes room for rational concerns. Worry is not always our enemy. You are right to worry about that mole on your leg that recently started getting larger. That worry will hopefully push you toward action, and you will get it checked by a physician. That is the function of emotion—to push us toward motion. Making a doctor's appointment goes in the IN basket. It is in your control. Whether that mole turns out to be malignant or not is not in your control. That thought goes in the OUT basket. You already considered that possibility when you made the appointment. Now breathe, and let go.

People who feel like they are in charge of their lives do not possess magic wands. They simply choose the focus of their efforts more wisely.

6.

Live by Your Values Instead of by Your Sensory Evaluations

There is no river like craving.

—BUDDHA *(Dhammapada #251)*

Values Are Now, Goals Are in the Future

It is possible to live without specific goals—life will then be like a walk in the park. But values are there at every step. Whether articulated or not, values accompany our journey because they determine how we walk.

It is possible to cheat on values to achieve a certain goal. According to Janine Driver in her book *You Can't Lie to Me*, nine out of ten people fudge their credentials or fabricate positive personal traits to get a job they want. Getting the job is a goal. Being truthful is a value. These days there are daily revelations about dishonesty at City Hall in Montreal. It turns out that many city employees have sacrificed their values (such as honesty) in order to achieve their goal (getting rich). They are among the unfortunate minority. According to Driver, only 20 percent of liars are ever caught.

Values must be kept in *mind* to be effective. That is why *mind*fulness helps us live according to our values. Many kinds of pressures conspire to deflect us from living according to our values. Stress and forgetfulness are two examples. But there is a third factor that can be even more powerful than those two. It is not often talked about because it does its work insidiously, behind the scenes. I'm talking about automatic sensory evaluations, or *feelings*, as they are sometimes called.

Twenty-six centuries ago, Buddha worked out an analysis of feeling that continues to surprise me at every turn with its insightfulness. However, what he meant by "feeling" (vedanā) is not the meaning we ordinarily ascribe to that word. In this context, he did not mean emotion—he meant a sensory evaluation we automatically form in response to a sense impression. The evaluation may be positive, negative, or neutral, and it accompanies every sensation we experience. It is simultaneous with a sensation. We do not first smell a mix of sesame and cinnamon and then decide that it smells good—we *smell* "yumm." This process no doubt helps an animal or a primitive organism to decide instantly whether to approach or avoid the source of a smell. It might save an animal's life by making it immediately run away from the smell of a predator, or it might direct a male toward the smell of a female in estrus, all without input from the thinking mind. The thinking process can be slow. Prey can escape while an animal debates the pros and cons of catching it for lunch. Vedanā happens instantaneously, like a reflex, and the animal acts. But without mindfulness, this way of responding may make us overweight, inebriated, addicted to various substances, or it may lead us to make inappropriate sexual choices.

Picture yourself at a family meal. Your partner's brother and his family have come over, and the dishes are lovingly prepared and particularly tasty. You notice that the serving platters are slowly being emptied as everyone takes second, and then third helpings and more. You look around the table and observe that everyone has a belly bulge; they had them even before they sat down to eat. Here is a situation that turns on its head the well-known passage from the Gospel of Matthew: the spirit is willing, but the flesh is weak.

Here the flesh is strong—the taste buds crave more and are getting their way but the spirit is weak. It is asleep or busy with something else—it has been lulled by the conversation. When our sensory evaluations are positive, we want the pleasant sensations to continue so we keep eating. We may be dimly aware of an inner voice that is saying, "You have had enough already," but often the sound of that voice gets drowned amid the clamor for more that is coming from the taste buds and the stomach.

On the other hand, when our automatic evaluations are negative, we try to avoid the source of discomfort. Furniture makers take advantage of this by promising the ultimate comfort in advertising a couch. They know that the sensors in our muscles can produce positive evaluations that trump the mind, which knows better. By a remarkable coincidence, "couch" rhymes with "slouch," and slouching invites back pain. In their wish to avoid discomfort, many people end up with worse trouble in the form of back pain. I have been one of them.

I occasionally face this in meditation groups, as someone not used to sitting straight in the usual meditation posture struggles to find the comfort of a couch on a meditation cushion. Just holding the back straight feels strange. Folding the legs creates extra tension, and participants get the feeling that stretching them out may be more comfortable. But this makes it almost impossible to hold the back straight! I explain that as long as we are alive, some amount of discomfort is inevitable. In our effort to attain the unattainable, we often trade one kind of discomfort for another; we trade the discomfort of sitting up straight for the discomfort of back pain, the discomfort of exercise for the discomfort of being out of shape. We trade the discomfort of mild hunger for the discomfort of the bloated feeling after eating too much, and the discomfort of boredom for the discomfort of being inebriated. And we complain.

Vedanā and Conditioning

Vedanā also creates conditioning. Like Pavlov's dogs salivating at the sound of a bell, certain sensations create craving and others, avoidance—all automatically. But on the bright side, as we become aware of this "packaging" of sensations with evaluations, we can resist—we can make conscious choices that reflect our values. Applied mindfulness means gaining freedom from a reflex type of reacting, and using that freedom to make deliberate decisions in tune with our values.

Buddhist psychology divides what we call "sensation" into two parts, with a third part, craving or aversion, that inevitably follows. What we ordinarily think of as "sensation" is called "contact"—contact between a sense object and our sense organs. This is accompanied by vedanā, which is the quality of a sensory experience, whether it is pleasant, unpleasant, or neutral. It is a bit like the Facebook term "Like," except that it is more complete; instead of the single choice of "Like," it has a wider spectrum of choices, which includes "Dislike" and "Neutral."

Western psychology often talks about sensation as if we can just hear things like a machine does and register a sound without making a distinction between, say, a note on a harp and chalk grating on a blackboard. They are both sensation. Buddhist psychology, on the other hand, says that when we listen, we do not just register a pressure wave like a microphone does, we also perceive a quality—always. Indeed, at times we are more conscious of the quality than of the sensation proper, as when we go into the kitchen and say, "I smell something delicious," without necessarily being aware of exactly what we are smelling—it could be stew, soup, or stir-fried vegetables. Then we go to the pot on the stove and lift the lid to look inside. And then we *see* something delicious. Again, we do not necessarily "see" things like a camera does, and may be unable to answer a question such as whether the dish we just looked at contains zucchini or not. But it looks delicious and we want some.

Vedanā can be more intense than the feeling of actual contact between a sense object and our sense organs. Vedanā is how we experience a sensation—as pleasant, unpleasant, or neutral—and it leads to the next step: craving if the sensation is experienced as pleasant, aversion if it is experienced as unpleasant, or indifference if it is experienced as neutral. All without any input from the thinking mind.

Buddhism invites us to be wary of craving and aversion. When the mind buys into sensory evaluations and accepts them as truth, we can become slaves to salt, sugar, and fat. We can develop a slouching addiction without even being aware of it. We can drink too much beer. We can buy a bigger and shinier car than we need.

If there are pleasant feelings associated with a sensation, they create a need, wish, or craving "behind our backs." This is not a rational, cognitive wish like, for example, the wish for a more peaceful world. This is a visceral craving that often overrides the rational mind. Buddhist psychology worked out the process involved many centuries ago, and depicted it in graphic terms in the Wheel of Life drawings. (A clear version of this image, as well as a discussion of it, appears in Thich Nhat Hanh's *The Heart of the Buddha's Teaching*.)

Our preferences can define who we are. We become "a beer drinker," for example. But it was the sensory evaluations (vedanā) that shaped our preferences. Thus, our sense of self as "a beer drinker" has been produced in part through an automatic process. But there is only a line in the sand between harmless or benevolent preference and destructive addiction. Substance use can change from recreational to addictive with deadly consequences.

We eat because of sensory evaluations, because eating creates pleasant sensations and helps us avoid the unpleasant sensations of hunger. But these same pleasant sensations are also part of our reward system—the system that creates addiction. Once we start, we continue to eat because we are unable to stop. We want the pleasant feelings to continue; what follows is weight gain, obesity, diabetes, and clogged arteries. There is the problem in a nutshell—survival, pleasure, and addiction are all related. Without mindfulness, sensory evaluation can turn an activity that is essential for survival, such as eating, into a cause of sickness.

And it can create stress along the way—the stress of not adhering to our values. We may value good health and attractiveness. We may instead be going inexorably in the direction of poor health and chubbiness. We are constantly reminded of this every time we get dressed, shop for clothes, go swimming, or just look in the mirror. The image in the mirror does not match the ideal picture we have of our body in our mental photo album. We experience the stress of feeling powerless and of being on a runaway train that is unable to stop. We are drowning in Buddha's river of craving.

Mindfulness of Sensory Evaluations

A morbidly obese doctor almost became Quebec's health minister during the last provincial election. An American president was almost impeached because of the complications resulting from his sexual impropriety. We may be puzzled when brilliant, accomplished people become slaves to their cravings, but sensory evaluation bypasses the conscious mind and intelligence. This is why mindfulness is so important. What we are unaware of can rule us. Awareness is power. It gives us the power of choice.

In the case of food, we have a narrow window of opportunity when conscious choice is possible. This is before we start eating. We can decide what and how much we are going to eat before we start, and develop strategies to stick to our decision. Once we start eating, sensory evaluation takes over and guides our fork. Intelligent, successful people have many skills, but they may not have the right skills. When cravings take over, it is not because of a defect of morality, IQ, or character, but because of a lack of mindfulness. In the good old days, parents did not want their teenage daughters to have sex before a certain age, so they chaperoned them. They wanted to prevent petting because once petting starts, "one thing leads to another." This is another way of saying that sensory evaluations take over, and we want the flow of pleasant feelings to continue.

SUGAR

Many of us are helpless in the face of sugar. Of the five basic tastes (sweet, bitter, sour, salty, and savory), sweetness activates most strongly the reward centers in the brain. In a 2007 report out of the University of Bordeaux in France, researchers discovered that intense sweetness trumps cocaine reward. When given the choice between sweetened water and intravenous cocaine injections, rats chose sweet water 94 percent of the time. They are like the daughter of an acquaintance who became obese and developed diabetes at the age of nineteen. This girl still gulps down a dozen or more soft drinks each day in spite of her doctor's advice. Yes, she is a real addict, but many others are not far behind. I still remember the ecstatic face of a five-year-old girl toting a huge bottle of Coke in a dusty street in the pueblo area of Tulum, Mexico. I remember the stories a friend who worked as a teacher in a native reserve in Ontario came back with: teenage mothers were putting Pepsi in the milk bottles of their infants.

Yet taming sugar cravings is possible. A small minority of us have done it. We do not sweeten our coffee or tea, we drink water rather than soft drinks, and we scour the grocery shelves for unsweetened yogurt. We are mindful that the positive sensory evaluation we get from consuming sweets does not mean that sugar is good for us in excess.

THINKING WITH YOUR MOUTH FULL

Mindfulness is up against a formidable adversary in our day. Junk food manufacturers work very hard to concoct foods that elicit the strongest positive evaluation from our taste buds. In *Salt Sugar Fat*, Michael Moss describes the extent of this effort. It reminded me of the Manhattan Project, the all-out effort to create the first atomic bomb during World War II: "Frito-Lay had a formidable research complex near Dallas, where nearly 500 chemists, psychologists and technicians conducted research that cost up to $30 million a year, and the science corps focused intense amounts of resources on questions of crunch, mouth feel, and aroma for each of these items. Their tools included a $40,000 device that simulated a chewing mouth to test and perfect the chips, discovering things like the perfect break point: people like a chip that snaps with about four pounds of pressure per square inch."

The obesity epidemic in the United States didn't just happen—it was carefully orchestrated. Food manufacturers know that sensory evaluation is not a rational procedure but a sensory one. Once they have the perfect formula for a winning taste, they know they can lead us, if not by the nose, then by the tongue, bypassing the mind entirely. Jonathan Kay, who reviewed *Salt Sugar Fat* for Canada's *National Post*, concluded: "We all know that processed foods are bad for us. But we're so powerless to resist their lab-concocted, cocaine-like lure that we can't stop eating them unless they are forcibly removed from our presence." The trouble is that there is no one assigned to this task of forcible removal. If you take it on at home with your children, partner, or guests, you may end up with sour feelings instead of gratitude.

Much better to awaken our capacity for mindfulness and let it handle the situation. The strategy of the junk food pushers is to bypass the mind. However, we have a number of resources at our disposal for fighting back:

- Look deeply to distinguish between hunger for food and hunger for sensory gratification. Which are you experiencing at this moment? Hunger for food is a need, and it can be satisfied. But hunger for pleasant sensations is a craving that happens automatically and continues unabated. We want more. When the stomach does its number and starts sending messages like, "If you do not eat right now, you will die. So drop everything and start eating. Eat whatever, but eat!", we can smile and talk back to it.

- The craving for pleasant sensations can be mollified in non-fattening ways: with interesting herbal teas, chewing gum, or plain water. You can also try strategies of distraction, such as going for a walk or putting on some music.

- Buy time. Count to ten slowly. Check your e-mail. Put the dishes away. The longer you delay gratification, the more chance that second thoughts will arise. With instant gratification, you do not give them a chance.

- Before you sit down for a meal, decide what you are going to eat and how much, and set it aside. You can still think rationally before starting to eat. Once the taste buds are engaged, vedanā takes over, and you continue eating just to keep the pleasant sensations flowing.

- Beware of the comfort food syndrome. As babies, we cried and our mothers gave us the breast or bottle. Every time a sad thought passes through our mind, even below the threshold of consciousness, there is a chance that we will crave food.

The strategies above can be modified to apply to things other than food, such as watching TV.

SATISFACTION OR STRESS?

We like tasty foods, pleasant music, pretty things, and nice fragrances. We spend good money for them—a bottle of Clive Christian's Imperial Majesty perfume costs $215,000. Even that old standby, Chanel No. 5, will set you back $1,850 in a large size. We spend lots of time shopping for pretty things. We eat for the joy of eating, often past the point of satiety. We have downloaded 16.5 billion songs just from the iTunes site—about 2.5 songs per person on the entire planet, including babies and senior citizens.

Do you see the connection? Buddha did.

We cling to sensory pleasures.

Sensory pleasures such as basking in the summer sun, savoring food, and getting high on birdsong are part of enjoying life. But there is a difference between this kind of healthy enjoyment of what is around us and the single-minded pursuit of sense pleasures. The first is part of being present—being here and in our senses. The second is mixed up with greed and craving. The first brings us satisfaction. The second often makes us stressed because we want more—we even cheat, swindle, lie, and steal to get more.

When the subject of sensory pleasures comes up, some people think that the Buddhist teachings are ambivalent. This is because on the one hand Jon Kabat-Zinn entitled one of his books *Coming to Your Senses* and Thich Nhat Hanh has a book with the title *Savor*, which refers to savoring your food. These books have a positive attitude toward sensory pleasures. On the other hand, there are other Buddhist teachings that present sense pleasures in a negative light. Which is right?

The key to this is simple. Coming to our senses is about enjoying what we find around us now. The admonitions against craving warn about pursuing sense pleasures relentlessly. It is the difference between enjoying our food and always craving more. It is the difference between a contented person and a hungry ghost. Indeed, while we lust after future pleasures, we can miss the enjoyment that is right under our noses.

Mindfulness at the Dining Table

Mealtimes can be tricky! If there are kids, they may be preoccupied with what they are doing and reluctant to stop and come to eat when called. They can also be reluctant to help with cleanup. Sometimes they are picky eaters, and all of the tensions around the "Eat your vegetables!" kind of parental requests can surface at that time and give rise to hard feelings. For a couple, the setting looks right for a discussion—two people facing each other at a table. Yet mealtime is more for celebration than for discussion, especially if the discussion centers on long-standing differences that can turn into an argument without warning. When that happens, the pleasure of eating evaporates, and the meal you prepared with loving care begins to taste like sawdust. Avoid emotionally charged issues at mealtime.

Another drawback to letting yourself get carried away by conversation or by your thoughts during a meal is that you may be eating too much or drinking too much without being aware of it.

All the more reason for bringing mindfulness to the dining table. Take a moment before the meal to let go of any outstanding thoughts or feelings, any worries you may have brought home from work, any resentment you may feel if you prepared the meal by yourself, and any discipline issues with children or things to be discussed with your partner. There is a time and a place for everything, and mealtime is not for these. It is also not the time for discourses about politics, the economy, or children's behavior. Food and the enjoyment of food are the main business at the dining table.

Food waste is another area where mindfulness can help. Collectively, we waste almost as much food as we eat. We pile more than we can eat on our plates, and then we scrape the leftovers into the garbage. If you like saying grace before meals, here is one that addresses this issue:

This food is the gift of the Earth and the result of much loving work.
Let us take as much as we need, and eat all we take.
Let us eat with a peaceful mind,
enjoy the company we keep, and savor every bite with gratitude.

A grace does not have to be said out loud every time. You can prepare the text on your computer, have it laminated, and make place mats. In our dining area I have a sign that reads NOURISH. It reminds me why I am there. In some ways "nourish" is a better word than "eat." It sidesteps issues like emotional eating, overeating, and unhealthy food. BREATHE is another appropriate word to display both in the kitchen and at the dinner table. In the context of mindfulness practice, "breathe" is shorthand for "Bring your attention from your thoughts to your breathing and to your body."

7.

Self-Regulation and Mindfulness

The Mind is its own place, and in itself can make
a heaven of hell, a hell of heaven.

—JOHN MILTON, *Paradise Lost*

Lucie, a seventh-grade teacher, was describing her day: "While I was writing on the blackboard I felt that something was going on in the back of the class. Sean had got up, gone over to another boy's desk, and was punching him. When I asked him what was happening, he replied, 'I had to hit him. He called me names.'"

Dellen, a mildly depressed and anxious history teacher, was talking about his failure to implement changes in his life such as exercising and eating healthier meals: "I know I should do these things. But I have no control over myself. In the past I have started programs but did not follow through. You know, some mornings I have trouble getting out of bed."

At first sight, Sean and Dellen seem to have opposite problems: one is having trouble *controlling* his impulses, while the other is having trouble *doing* what he wants to do. Could these two problems be related? In fact, Dellen also has trouble controlling his impulses—he smokes, and although he would like to stop, when he gets the urge he feels as powerless over his actions as Sean. How much control do we have over our actions?

Dellen thinks he doesn't have any, but as I told him, that is just another thought. As he fuses with that thought, he is convinced of it. Yet he does manage to go to work every morning, and he comes regularly to our sessions. That's a contradiction he has not considered.

Getting out of bed in the morning is tricky. I once saw a T-shirt on a teenage cashier at the local convenience store that read: "I got out of bed this morning. What else do you want?" I could read her daily struggles with her parents about getting up in time to catch the school bus on that T-shirt.

We think of getting out of bed in terms of what we can do once we are up. We rarely consider what we are leaving behind. Yet rolling around in bed in the morning is a sensuous experience. Our bare feet encounter each other and delight in each other's company. Just being horizontal instead of vertical is less stressful for the organism. As we stretch and turn, the feel of the sheets against our skin is delicious. The sensory evaluation that is the subject of chapter 6 kicks in, and we want the pleasant sensations to continue. Add a bit of daydreaming and the sense of freedom from obligations, and it gets even better. As I was discussing this chapter with my partner, who works as a consultant in the supplements section of a large health food store, she laughed and told me about the young man who came in that day looking for a supplement to help him get out of bed in the mornings.

Dellen and the teenage cashier have lots of company.

The Anatomy of Control

Sean's teacher would like him to have more self-control, but neither Sean nor the teacher is clear about what needs to be controlled. When someone calls him names, Sean gets upset. We can grant him that he feels that he has no control over his emotion. What he needs to know is that he can feel "hot under the collar" and feel the impulse to punch his classmate without actually doing it. He may have no control over his feelings or impulses—especially given his young age—but even at his age, he does have control over his behavior. He demonstrated this control when he waited for the teacher to turn her back to the class to write on the blackboard before he punched the other boy. If an older and much bigger boy had called him names, Sean most likely would not have tried to punch him.

The Telephone Call

Consider the following scenario.

You are having a heated argument with a member of your family—you are in the middle of an acrimonious exchange, feeling angry, and perhaps even yelling at each other.

Just then the telephone rings. It is a business call from a client. He has a question about an important contract that you were hoping he would sign.

Suddenly your voice changes—it is now full of warm concern. You start listening attentively, really listening so that you can understand his hesitations and address them appropriately. You are ready to make concessions and compromises. You think of, and suggest, alternate wordings to rephrase problem clauses so that they will be mutually acceptable.

In the blink of an eye you have become a different person, and in many ways this new person is quite the opposite of the first one. Where the first one was all output and no input, this new person listens. Where the first one was using harsh words, this new person is kind and polite. Where the first one was talking loudly and interrupting, this new person waits until the other stops talking and replies in a normal tone of voice.

Your spouse or whomever you were arguing with before the phone rang is now watching in amazement. . . .

Everyday life is full of examples like this that show that we have more control over our behavior than we sometimes like to believe.

Anger

Anger is probably the emotion most often responsible for loss of control. Like other emotions, anger incites us to action, but what kind of action? Anger is often accompanied by an urge to harm. We want to harm the object of our anger, but sometimes any object will do. The door may get kicked or slammed, and a person may get angry with the boss and take it out on his or her family. Mindfulness makes it possible to be aware of our urges so that instead of acting them out in damaging ways, we redirect them toward compassionate and beneficial deeds.

Many changes in the world may have started with a feeling of anger. These include wars but also the founding of nongovernment organizations that promote women's rights.

Losing Sight of Your Values

Before it took on the connotation of "being in the moment," the word "mindfulness" meant remembering, or keeping in mind. It is still used in that sense, notably by the Dalai Lama when he defines mindfulness as "the ability to bring our accumulated wisdom to bear upon this and every moment." Strong emotions can make us lose that ability. "A crime of passion" refers to killing one's wife or her lover, especially if they are caught in bed. It implies that rage, anger, jealousy, and other strong emotions have completely taken over the mind, and mindfulness of the sixth commandment ("Thou shalt not murder") has disappeared from consciousness. This is also known as temporary insanity. Temporary insanity has been used successfully as a legal defense in the past, but it is no longer considered as compelling.

Strong emotions are not the only reason for losing sight of one's values. Alcohol is another. The typical Saturday night murder is often a deadly combination of the two. "Saturday night" means "alcohol" to many, and alcohol is a well-known antagonist of mindfulness—Buddha made absti-nence from alcohol a condition for joining his community. When alcohol is paired with anger or impulsiveness, mindfulness can go out the window.

I DON'T GET ANGRY, I GET EVEN

Here's an expression that attests to our control over our actions. Who-ever came up with the phrase, however, was confusing the feeling of anger with the impulsive kind of action we often associate with anger. "I get angry, but I don't act impulsively. I plan my actions so that they will be effective," may be a better way to put it. The character who made it up did get angry despite her denial—otherwise she would not spend time and en-ergy devising ways of taking sweet revenge. She's the type who does not rant and rave. She just gets up quietly in the middle of the night and lets the air out of your tires.

IS GETTING EVEN THE ONLY OPTION?

Here's a story Amy told in one of our groups. Doug, Amy's older son, had always been an underperformer in school. The previous semester he had failed two courses and dropped out of college. Since then, he had been liv-ing in his old basement room in Amy's suburban bungalow. He had tried a string of dead-end jobs, and did not last long in any of them. It seemed like he had ho higher ambitions than playing computer games and pumping gas at the local garage.

Amy was awakened one night at 3 a.m. by the familiar sounds of Doug's computer games. She immediately felt furious—her anger at Doug's lazy behavior had been brewing for a long time. She put on her housecoat and headed toward the door with the intention of giving him a piece of her mind.

Then she stopped. She had remembered the mindfulness teachings about not acting in anger. When we act in anger we may say or do things we later regret. We can create more problems than we solve, and we create extra stress.

Amy took off her housecoat and went back to bed.

This made possible a heart-to-heart conversation with Doug the next day in which Amy used all her skills as a school counselor to help him. And her relationship with her son was strengthened instead of damaged.

REMEMBERING THE REST OF YOU

We are not as one-sided as we may appear when we are "temporarily insane," or suffering from momentary paralysis after the alarm goes off. We all have compassion and empathy in our hearts. We all have things that we want to do once we make it out of bed. But we are blinded by vedanā, or sensory evaluations, as described in chapter 6, or by our emotions. If I always waited until I *felt* like going to the gym, I would only go occasionally. I would miss the benefits of regular exercise. It is unfortunate but true—when I most need the exercise, that's when I feel the least like going. Sometimes we do something because we feel like doing it. The feeling comes first. At other times doing comes first. We just start, and the activity creates its own momentum and soon we are totally into it.

MANY LAYERS OF MIND

Picture a dryer full of clothes rotating in slow motion. As the drum turns, certain items come to the top and others disappear from view. The mind is like that—thoughts, images, memories, and mental states are constantly tumbling. Our feelings are created by what's on top. The other items are temporarily hidden from view, although they are still there somewhere. They are not driving our feelings for the moment. Starting an activity when we are not particularly driven to is like reaching for a shirt that is temporarily at the bottom of the pile. When we reach for it, we bring it to the top, and then it starts to drive feelings. We do not have to wait for the shirt to appear at the top of the pile by itself. We can reach for it. When musicians play a show, it is not because by some magical coincidence they all suddenly felt like playing music at the scheduled moment.

SELF-REGULATION

At any given time, we are a bundle of likes, dislikes, discomfort, longings, feelings, values, goals, enthusiasm, reticence, perhaps some aches and pains, and even some heartache as well. When we get up in the morning, this whole bundle gets up. When we go on a date, this whole bundle goes. If you let some discomfort hold you back, the rest of the bundle suffers. Your longings suffer. Your values and goals will be in distress. If you let fear stop you from moving forward, your whole day or evening will stall. If you do that systematically, your life will stall. In trying to avoid extra stress, you create more stress—you create regret and frustration. In meditation, we sit and watch as everything in the bundle that we call our "self" slowly tumbles in and out of awareness. We become intimate with all the contents of the bundle. We are then less likely to take the item that is currently on top of the bundle, like the emotion we are currently experiencing, as representing the whole self.

This enhances self-regulation skills.

EACH OF US IS A BUNDLE

We should be glad that every person has a degree of egoism—otherwise somebody else would have to take care of them.

Complete altruism can be equally problematic—there is a story about the modern-day Indian guru Amma "the Hugging Guru." She was born into a poor, low-caste family. As a child, Amma was always giving away whatever valuables her family owned, which prompted her father to tie her to a tree!

RESISTING THE SIRENS' SONG

In meditation we not only watch our states of mind and emotions as they arise and pass, but we also watch the urges they create, without acting on them. Meditation is a little bit like the experience of Odysseus as his boat passed within earshot of the island of the Sirens. Odysseus had many adventures on his way home from the Battle of Troy, and he knew that the Sirens' song was irresistible—there were stories of sailors who had heard it and threw themselves into the sea in an effort to swim ashore, but they perished because the rocks and currents in that spot were particularly treacherous. However, as his boat approached the Sirens' island, Odysseus became curious as to what their song sounded like. So he asked his crew to tie him to the mast with instructions not to untie him until the boat was well past the island. All the crew wore earplugs. Odysseus heard the Sirens' song and felt the longing but could not act on his impulse to jump into the sea.

Like Odysseus in this story, when we sit in meditation we may feel urges, discomfort, or restlessness, yet we are "tied" to the meditation cushion, and we do not act. We learn to just observe our urges and feelings. Mindfulness is not denying or ignoring our feelings—it is a commitment not to act on them mindlessly.

✦

Waking Up in the Morning

Waking up this morning, I see the blue sky, I join my
hands in thanks for the many wonders of life.

—THICH NHAT HANH

On which side of the bed do you usually get up?

The right side, or the wrong side?

This is too important a matter to leave to chance. If you start your day already stressed, it's going to go downhill from there. Reading this verse each morning will call up positive feelings of appreciation, gratitude, wonder, and even awe at the miracle of life, and get your day started on the right foot.

Here is another Thich Nhat Hanh quotation that is a nice complement to the one above:

Waking up this morning, I smile. Twenty-four brand-new hours are before me. I vow to live fully in each moment and to look at all beings with eyes of compassion.

Here, good feelings of anticipation and compassion are supplemented with a physical expression of them: a smile.

In her book *Positivity*, Barbara L. Fredrickson documents with study after study that good feelings expand our vision and make us see more possibilities. They also make us more successful in life: happy people not only see more possibilities, but more possibilities are opened to them.

What we see of the sky is not always blue. Nevertheless, the blue sky is always there above the clouds. Can you see the sky above the clouds, or do you only see the clouds?

Lovingly format or handwrite these short verses and put them in a strategic place where you can see them as you open your eyes in the morning. Waking up with positive feelings is an excellent complement, or even an alternative, to caffeine. I see what caffeine does to people when I look at how they drive to work in the morning! According to Professor James Lane of Duke University Medical Center, even moderate caffeine consumption makes a person react like they are having a stressful day.

Waking up with this verse will have a gentler effect on your morning activities.

8.

Choose Your Passions
and Obsessions

King Solomon got carried away
and collected 1,000 wives
and watched his treasures fade away
like picked flowers . . .
Krishna had a different disposition
—I like his position—
he danced, played the flute, and moved on
leaving behind fond memories
and intense longing . . .
the Garden is a treasure trove—
sunshine like liquid amber
dewdrops like pearls
spring flowers fresh
with each creature hugging the others' beauty
The self that wants to own it all
is already in exile from its spirit.

—J. E.

If you have ever been to a zoo, you have likely seen a tiger pacing its cage with one thought in its mind: to escape into freedom. The Dalai Lama quotes Patrul Rinpoche at the beginning of his book *How to See Yourself as You Really Are*:

> *When starting to practice, be eager like a deer*
> *trapped in a pen seeking to get out.*

The same thoughts keep arising automatically in such a one-track mind. When this happens, I think it's fair to refer to them as obsessions. In psychological literature, we encounter "obsession" mostly in the context of the obsessive-compulsive disorder, which has no redeeming, creative, or benign side. But a passionate obsession that makes us think about something all the time and be preoccupied by it constantly can have a positive side. It is a state of mind felt by lovers, composers, poets, and creative scientists like Einstein. Passion refers to the quality and intensity of your preoccupation. Obsession also takes account of its quantity.

To come back to that trapped deer and the caged tiger, their obsession with getting free is a positive one. So is the obsession to become cancer-free in someone who has just received that dreaded diagnosis. You can bet that she is preoccupied with the thought of regaining her health. In contrast, an obsession with revenge is not positive. Neither was the obsessive hatred that drove terrorists to attack the World Trade Center.

"Special people with talent." This is how many people view musicians. I know better. I have spent seventeen years hanging out with them and playing Irish accordion at weekly sessions. I would not say that possession of talent was the dominant characteristic of all my erstwhile musical companions. Yes, a few of them were especially talented, and we all looked up to them. But many more were average, and a few less than average—a typical bell curve kind of distribution. I notice a similar distribution of talent among the artists who display their work at the neighborhood coffeehouses and restaurants I go to, and among the craftspeople who rent tables at annual Christmas fairs. What characterized my musical companions above all was passion and obsession. They were all "crazy" about Irish music.

One creative artist whose talent matches his obsession is Leonard Cohen. In response to interviewer Paul Zollo's question "Do you find that your mind is always working on songs, even when you're not actively working?" he answered, "Yes. But I'm actively working on songs most of the time. Which is why my personal life has collapsed. Mostly I'm working on songs."

And again:

"I worked months and months on 'Suzanne.' It's just a matter of intensity. I was still able to juggle stuff: a life, a woman, a dream, other ambitions, other tangents. At a certain point I realized I only had one ball in my hand, and that was The Song. Everything else had been wrecked or compromised and I couldn't go back, and I was a one-ball juggler."

Despite the personal price he has had to pay, Leonard Cohen's passionate obsession has a positive side—it has brought him personal satisfaction, and his songs have enriched the lives of other people. In contrast, King Solomon's one thousand wives must have brought him mostly headaches and extra stress. I can just picture him shopping for greeting cards on Valentine's Day! And all those frustrated young women living in close quarters may have needed frequent workshops on nonviolent communication.

The problem with allowing yourself to become obsessed with possessions (and women were regarded as possessions by rich and powerful men in days of old) is twofold: (1) you can only enjoy your possessions one at a time, and (2) those possessions have a life of their own and demand your attention. The tables are turned, and without realizing it you become the servant of your possessions.

Imelda Marcos may have had three thousand pairs of shoes, but she could only wear one pair at a time. And shoes are often uncomfortable the first time you wear them. So she signed up for three thousand days of torture. And you need a room (not just a closet) for three thousand pairs of shoes. If you also have a comparable number of sweaters and blouses, you would need a whole house. And each day you have to walk over to that house and look through three thousand pairs of shoes and three thousand five hundred sweaters to choose what you want to wear that day. You also need to vacuum the house and dust the shelves regularly. I get exhausted just thinking about it.

I remember the day of my own vestimentary awakening. That day I switched from thinking of clothes as objects to seeing them in terms of their use. You can become obsessed with pretty objects and want to collect them. But objects also take up room and get in your way. When I started thinking of clothes in terms of their use, I realized that a few of each item is enough.

Incidentally, thinking of the function instead of the object clarifies one's approach in other areas as well. Cupcakes? Think function. Do you need a pretty cupcake or do you need to take care of your hunger so that you can spend a productive afternoon? Cars? Think function again. Do you need transportation or do you need a shiny object on wheels? If what you crave is the shiny object on wheels, you naturally want the shiniest and the cutest one. Those are expensive. When you choose in terms of function, you choose more rationally because you are not tempted by the appearances of objects. If you were taking the bus to go downtown, would you refuse to get on one because it was not the latest model?

Thinking in terms of objects activates greed and possessiveness. In contrast, thinking in terms of use and function activates pathways of simplicity and elegance. When you think of objects, big is beautiful and more appears to be better. When you think of function, small is beautiful and downsizing makes sense.

Thomas Cathcart and Daniel Klein have a joke about this in their book *Plato and a Platypus Walk into a Bar* . . . :

Salesman: Ma'am, this vacuum cleaner will cut your work in half.

Customer: Terrific! Give me two of them.

Passions That Redeem the Day

The Buddhist tradition is not particularly object-friendly. It is experience- and action-friendly. Things disintegrate or lose their separateness under the gaze of the Buddha.

A table? You can see a tree in it, and in the tree, sunshine, rain, and soil.

You and me? We are an ecosystem consisting of ten times as many microbes as human cells. We are impermanent and not separable from the air we breathe and the water we drink.

Money? Its value is entirely dependent on the government that issues it and market conditions. "You can't eat money," as a Native American proverb says.

In return, our behavior, our actions (or karma), the intentions behind them, and their moral quality describe who we are and who we are becoming. To come back to Leonard Cohen, when he was asked how a song begins in his mind, he answered, "It begins with an appetite to discover my self-respect. To redeem the day. So the day does not go down in debt." There is no redeeming quality to buying three thousand pairs of shoes for yourself.

Choose Your Obsession

It may appear as if our obsessions choose us instead of the other way around, because they are fueled by our automatic thoughts. But what fuels automatic thoughts? You might answer that they just happen, like sunshine. But sunshine does not just happen. It is fueled by nuclear reactions at the surface of the sun. What fuels our automatic thoughts?

Greed and a wish to redeem the day were the fuels in the examples above, but obviously this varies from person to person. Fear, food, sex, shopping, desire for success, babies, a wish for dominance, self-expression, self-actualization, and a desire to help others are a few common ones.

Take a minute now and reflect. What are some of the predominant themes in your automatic thoughts? You may like to sit in meditation for a few minutes and then write them down. Or you may like to imagine that you are being interviewed like Leonard Cohen was.

Then, working backward, you can become aware of what fuels your thoughts.

Doing this exercise will free you from the robotic feeling of being led by irresistible forces.

Yes, you can change the course of your automatic thoughts and your obsessions. Remember, you may have been obsessed with Barbie dolls once, or with toy cars and trucks. You got over that, didn't you? You may say that this was an inevitable consequence of brain growth with age. But growth happens at any age. The brain retains its plasticity all through life. Many people grow and mature all through life despite what my refrigerator magnet says: "You are only young once, but you can stay immature forever."

Outgrowing an Obsession

One can outgrow an obsession through life experiences and by the natural processes of maturing. One can also do it with focus and concentration. Essential to that is what we may call "soul searching." This implies looking deep into oneself. As I repeat several times throughout this book, one of the first and basic functions of mindfulness is recognition. We can recognize our most intimate mental processes through the process of deep looking.

Visualize yourself as a lake. You want to see deep into the lake. You can't do this if the surface is agitated by the wind or waves. You can only do it if the surface is calm. Calming the mind is the first step in meditation. Bits and pieces of thoughts float about on the surface of consciousness without much consequence. Leonard Cohen describes this well in the course of the interview I quoted earlier: "My immediate realm of thought is bureaucratic and like a traffic jam." That state of mind is not conducive to insight.

The winds of emotion may be agitating the surface of your lake, or left-over waves from disturbances that happened earlier:

Thoughts come at me like waves on the lake—
a boat passes, and circles of water advance to tell me
The wind blows, and an army of tiny crests race with the news.

—J. E.

In the evening, when the boat traffic stops and the wind dies, the surface of the lake becomes like a mirror. Then the lake faithfully reflects outer reality—clouds, seagulls, trees, or whatever else is above it. It also becomes transparent if you look closely: you can see if the bottom is sandy or full of plants—you can see the inner reality of the lake.

Meditation masters in the Buddhist tradition have calmed the surface and looked deep into the lake of their souls. They have found many things there: love, hate, compassion, anger, envy, altruism, deceitfulness, honesty, confusion, joy, and more. They have treasured what was beautiful, and brought them to the surface.

Visualize yourself as a skin diver, swimming along and contemplating all these qualities lying like different colored pebbles or shells at the bottom of the lake of your heart. Which ones would you like to leave lying there and which ones would you like to pick up and bring to the surface? Which ones would you like to collect as trophies and display on your coffee table at home? Would you pick up confusion or joy, hate or love?

What I just described is the way of mindfulness meditation—calming the lake of your mind so you can see the bottom, becoming aware of the various mental states that lie there, and consciously choosing to cultivate positive ones by contemplating them often.

Things happen quite differently without mindfulness meditation.

The surface is agitated so you do not see what lies below.

You do not choose. Instead, the storms of everyday life churn up the lake and bring up different things to the surface. It could be hatred one moment and jealousy the next. Think of the flotsam you sometimes see floating on a muddy lake—a Coke bottle, a candy wrapper . . . This is our ordinary consciousness. And we accept this, just like we accept the Coke bottles and candy wrappers floating on our real lakes. And just like some of these things do not add beauty to the scenery, some of the things that lie at the bottom of our consciousness do not bring us happiness. Instead, they bring us stress.

I often remember this sign I saw on the wall of the Franciscan monastery in Sucre, Bolivia: *El mejor cosmético para la belleza es la felicidad.*

"The best cosmetic for beauty is happiness."

Not stress.

✦

Reminders or Visual Mantras

When I first went to Plum Village, I saw a calligraphy in Thich Nhat Hanh's distinctive hand that asked WHAT ARE YOU DOING? The obvious answer may be something like, "I'm standing around." But there is more to it than that. It is a trick question, for the body and the mind may be doing different things. Everyone can see that you are standing around. No need to ask. But what is the mind doing? Is the mind there with the body, or is it doing something else? That question was designed to bring awareness.

Our current mental habits took years to develop. We need reminders and time to change them. Here are some words and phrases you can display around your living space and work space to keep your mindfulness practice fresh.

Sometimes a sign can become part of the furniture, and we stop paying attention to it. Anytime you feel that a sign is not working for you, you can replace it or change its place.

Here are some reminders of the type you will find at Plum Village.

These visual mantras appear here without special formatting. Feel free to rewrite them on your computer using a font and size you prefer. You can also decorate them to your liking, or write them out by hand. That way, they will be more meaningful for you. I have a collection of short mantras written on beach stones of various sizes. I used correcting fluid to write with because it comes in a bottle with a brush.

If you are writing on paper, felt pens work well, especially if you find one with the tip cut to a 45-degree angle. You can find other reminders like these on the Internet. You can start by doing a search for Thich Nhat Hanh's calligraphy.

PEACE IS EVERY STEP

JUST BREATHE, EVERYTHING WILL BE ALL RIGHT.

PRACTICE MINDFULNESS

A SMILE WITH EVERY BREATH

HAPPINESS IS HERE AND NOW

I HAVE ALREADY ARRIVED, I'M ALREADY AT HOME

SMILE, LIFE IS A MIRACLE

THE MIND IS A CLEAR BLUE SKY

HAPPINESS MAKES YOU BEAUTIFUL

THERE IS NO WISDOM WITHOUT LOVE.

On the next two pages you'll find examples of how you can format each of these to look attractive. You can photocopy them.

"Breathing in,
I come back to an island of
peace in my heart"

I have already arrived,
I'm already at home

9.
Coming to Acceptance

There were tears in Lori's eyes as she recounted the story of her mother: "She did everything right—she ate well, exercised, and took care of herself. She is a beautiful woman. She does not deserve to get Alzheimer's." Lori is an attractive brunette in her fifties, and as she spoke it became clear that part of her distress was for herself. "I panic when I can't remember a name. Am I going to end up like her?"

In my courses I meet people who have some life issue that is causing them extra stress. Sometimes it is something going wrong at work, sometimes a problem with a child, and sometimes, as in Lori's case, a worrisome situation with a parent. Often there is an underlying feeling that "life is not supposed to be like this. Everything is supposed to go right. Doesn't it, for other people?"

I recounted the story of Kisa Gotami to Lori.

Gotami, a contemporary of the Buddha, was a young mother of a baby boy. She woke up one morning to find that her baby was not breathing. To put things in context, she was probably a teen bride in India, where a woman's worth was measured by her ability to bear male children. Women who didn't bear a son were sometimes treated with disrespect and even cruelty by their husbands and in-laws. Like Lori's, Gotami's grief was likely tinged with distress for herself.

The story recounts that she was overcome with grief. Not wanting to accept the obvious, she ran in all directions—to the marketplace and to her neighbors—asking if they had some medicine to cure her baby. Others saw that the baby was beyond help and sadly shook their heads. One person wisely suggested that she go to see the Buddha. She ran to him and, sobbing, repeated her story. I can picture the Buddha listening with compassion, not only to her words, but also to her state of mind and attitude.

"I can cure your child," he said. "There is a medicine that I can make that will cure him. Just bring me some mustard seeds. But take care: these mustard seeds must come from a home where no family member has died."

More context: to this day, Indians use mustard seeds like we use onions. They fry mustard seeds in oil first and then add vegetables or whatever else goes into the dish. Far from being an exotic food, mustard seeds were a common staple in Indian kitchens.

Also, twenty-six centuries ago, before the age of real estate agents, people did not sell their houses after an average of seven years, as they do today. Extended families lived in ancestral homes generation after generation. As Gotami went from house to house and repeated Buddha's request, she was met with one sad tale after another: a parent, child, spouse, or other close relative had died in every house.

I can picture Gotami's "Why me?" attitude slowly eroding as the day wore on. Loss was not something that happened only to her. It happened to everyone. It was a universal experience as common as mustard seeds. People learned to live with it.

The story goes on to recount that at the end of the day she sat by the roadside and reflected awhile. Then she walked to the village cemetery and lovingly buried her infant. As I told this story to Lori, I was keenly aware that knowing about the suffering of other people does not diminish our own. It only makes acceptance more likely. We no longer think that this is *not* the way things should be, or that fate has singled us out for harsh treatment. Rather, this is the way things are.

Kisa Gotami could be considered the patron saint of acceptance and commitment. She exemplified not only acceptance in her life but also commitment to her new values. Buddhist history recounts that she later became an arhat, a teacher of wisdom.

◆   ◆   ◆

There are two aspects to stress. One is the actual stressful event. Kisa Gotami's story underlines that such events happen to everyone. The second aspect is the story we weave around the stressful event.

Thanks to her encounter with the Buddha, Gotami told herself two very different stories about her loss, both in the course of a single day.

A One-Sided Coin?

Birth and death have driven the engine of evolution—without them we would not have evolved to become modern humans and to complain about our losses. Without death, we may have a Cro-Magnon for a neighbor, a true senior citizen at the ripe old age of forty thousand years. We might encounter others like him on the highway, as they drive to the local Walmart to shop for bows and arrows. Sickness, old age, and death are part of the bargain. They are like the "I agree" button that we click on without much thought when we download an application. We, and our parents, have clicked on that button at birth for generations. For what is the alternative? As on a computer, that button does not signal acceptance of all conditions but a wish to go ahead. Acceptance may come later as we read the small print and discover all the constraints and requirements that go with the privilege of being here. When we are young, we coast along blissfully ignorant of that small print: old age, sickness, and death are things that happen to others, aren't they? As an old joke says, "I plan to live forever. So far everything is going according to plan." Many of us continue on with that attitude for as long as we can—without getting the joke.

Death gives meaning to life.

Here's how:

We tend to equate happiness with goal achievement. However, when associated with goal achievement, happiness, and its close cousin, contentment, quickly advance to the end of the rainbow. They are seen as feelings we will experience only when our goals are realized—later, not now. There is no doubt that goals are important; but awareness of sickness, old age, and death urges us to temper the satisfaction of goal achievement with the enjoyment of the present moment.

Coming to terms with old age, sickness, and death is not an exercise in morbidity. "Saving time" is a misnomer. We cannot "save" time in the same sense that we can save money. There is no "time bank." We cannot put it away to use later. If we "spend" time, it is gone. If we "save" it, it is also gone. If we do not consider this as part of the equation, our values will be skewed. The happiness that we postpone will slowly become more and more out of reach.

Think of days as pages in a coloring book: the pages are there in the book as black-and-white outlines, and it is up to us to fill them with beautiful colors.

The body scan is a way of coming to the here and now, of getting in touch with what is going on in our bodies now. So is walking meditation. We often walk in order to get somewhere. The here and now sensations of the body are discounted in favor of a vision of where we want to end up. That is where walking meditation differs from our usual way of walking. Walking meditation is a mindfulness practice based on being present. Being present to enjoy the moment is an essential skill, for without it we will be unable to enjoy the future either. When that future arrives, we will still be thinking of another future, still not in the moment. Sacrificing the present for a future is a slippery mental habit. If we feel more at home in our thoughts than in our body, we will always be more at home in the past or in the future, for they are made of thoughts. The present moment is made of sensations. So is joy. Sensations are transformed into memories and thoughts as the moment passes. Living in the moment is living in real time.

See What Is Right

Once we arrive in the present moment, another hurdle appears, for like the rosebush, the present moment is made of thorns as well as flowers.

"Life is both wonderful and terrible," says Thich Nhat Hanh. In the poem "The Good News," he exhorts us to focus on the wonderful:

The good news is that your child is there before you,
and your arms are available:
hugging is possible.

In the end, it is a choice to focus on beauty and not ugliness, on joy and not sadness. The birds have made that choice and enliven our world with their exuberance every moment. Not only birds but all nature. Flowers may express their joy in being alive differently from birds, but they are every bit as exuberant. A dandelion, for example, often displays its radiance even in uninspiring places, such as a patch of soil right next to a sidewalk.

Thich Nhat Hanh gets more specific in another poem:

A tree is dying in my garden.
I see it, but I also see other trees that are still vigorous and thriving,
And I am thankful.

Indeed, this is true even in my small yard. The ash tree in the front has fallen victim to the emerald ash borer and is already half dead. But thankfully there are a dozen other trees that are gloriously alive. The situation is similar in my partner's garden—the slugs always damage some plants, but the garden continues to produce tasty vegetables year after year.

Urban Culture

Another hurdle to appreciating the present moment is our urban lifestyle.

For better or for worse, most of us live in the city now. We may make occasional forays into the countryside, but these remain visits or vacations. For most of us our home, our work, our heart is in the city, and sooner or later we return there. The world of the city is not made of nature, of trees and vegetable gardens, but of culture, songs, TV programs, and movies. In the city, our contact with nature is secondhand. We mostly see life as it is reflected in literature—in books and magazines—and on TV and the Internet.

Our major cultural institutions such as museums, symphony halls, theaters, and opera houses are no different from pop culture in this respect— they also present us with takes on the natural world. They offer us the visions of artists. Some of these artists found happiness, but others lived unhappy lives and reflect their unhappiness in their art. Seeing this unhappy art officially sanctioned by governments and universities may give us the impression that there is something important there, something to be studied and learned, perhaps even absorbed and imitated. However, these artists attained prominence mostly through a dazzling mastery of their craft, not through their wisdom or ability to find and reflect happiness. Their personal lives may in fact be examples to be avoided, their art visions to stay away from. Many are not secular prophets but rather pied pipers.

Examples abound. One Kurt Cobain song consists mostly of the words "rape me" repeated over and over.

And Lil Wayne's "Money on my Mind" shouts obscenities and declares: "Dear Mr. Toilet I'm the shit."

"Official culture" also provides many unfortunate examples. Goethe's *Sorrows of Young Werther*, in which the hero of the story kills himself after failing to win the love of a young woman who is engaged to someone else, influenced other unstable and confused young men to follow his example. By some estimates, as many as two thousand men committed copycat suicides after reading this book.

Much better to go with Bob Marley. He has a wonderful way of being upbeat without being aggressive. In "Three Little Birds," one of my favorites, he describes the joy of getting up with the rising sun and finding three little birds singing on his doorstep. The birds are singing,

"Don't worry 'bout a thing,
'Cause every little thing gonna be all right."

Just reading these lines relaxes me now.

You can also search for "It's a Wonderful World" on YouTube. You will most likely be smiling by the end of the song.

My purpose here is not to compare "high" culture with pop culture. My purpose is to point out that one does not become happy by watering negative emotions. Urban culture thrives on the written word and the sung word. Many artists are not preoccupied with the effect their work has on the minds of their public. In their search for success and money, they often spread around attitudes you would not want to emulate.

"You Belong to Me," a Jason Wade song, was on the airwaves often in its heyday. It describes some beautiful scenery such as the pyramids along the Nile, the marketplace in Algiers, and a tropical island at sunrise, only to remind the woman in question that wherever she is, and whatever she may be doing, she is to keep constantly in mind that "you belong to me." What does it promote? As possessive an attitude toward women as you will find in the darkest recesses of a fundamentalist's mind. Only the chains are missing.

Be Careful What Messages You Absorb

We are swimming in a culture soup. The media is our environment now, more than forests and meadows. Traditional Buddhist teaching emphasizes watering the seeds of positive states of mind so that we can move in the direction of happiness and contentment. But the media are doing some seed watering of their own. And the gardener is losing control, because the marketplace controls the watering hose now.

As I watch young men and women with headphones everywhere, I wonder what values they are soaking up from their iPods. Are they enjoying their urban paradise, or drowning in an urban hell?

✦

Give Your iPod a Makeover

Music is not neutral. It is not "just" music.

In fact, nothing is neutral. Painting your walls and ceiling black is not neutral. It is not "just" interior decoration. It has an effect on your mood and your life. And some music is as black as black paint.

In this exercise, my focus is on songs, and songs are about words. You can find relaxing and uplifting instrumental music relatively easily. Don Campbell's *The Mozart Effect* can inspire you on your search.

Music is a sacred practice. Singing is part of many spiritual traditions. You will hear practice songs at Plum Village and other Thich Nhat Hanh practice centers. I wrote and recorded many of them. My collection is entitled *A Basket of Plums*, and is available as an e-book from Parallax Press (Parallax.org). It has forty-two songs and a foreword by Thich Nhat Hanh. What makes this collection interesting is that the sheet music for all the songs is included so that you can sing along. The music you listen to should nourish a sense of well-being. The songs in the *Basket of Plums* collection are designed with this in mind. They are songs to accompany mindfulness practice.

When it comes to music, we all have our preferences. There are many songs in the marketplace with words that are compatible with mindfulness practice, and many others that aren't. Do not get seduced by lovely melodies and enchanting rhythms. The words of many songs are toxic. Those lovely melodies and enchanting rhythms will imprint the words on your consciousness subliminally. Check out the lyrics on the

Internet. Do not "adopt" a song unless you can relate to the words and feel that they are in harmony with your values. As documented in the movie *The Singing Revolution*, the Estonians liberated themselves from Soviet occupation without the loss of a single life, through the power of song. You can harness the same power to help liberate yourself from excess stress.

You do not want songs on your iPod that add to your stress.

PART THREE

Change

10.

A Chance Encounter

I met Change in my thirties, while traveling in Mexico. I was staying at Don Armando's cabañas in Tulum, a string of thatched-roof cabins on the white sands of the Caribbean.

"Hi, I'm Joseph," I said, as we were both waiting for laundry.

"I am Change," she replied.

I had already known a few women who had been new-age babies—I knew Flower and Crystal. But Change was new to me, and together with the bougainvillea and the palm trees, she and her name became part of the enchantment of that place. I left that encounter in a bit of a daze, suddenly awake to the fact that the sunset I gazed at every evening was also change, together with the surf and the wind. I was also change, but it had taken me this moment to see it clearly. Walking back, I realized that I now knew why I liked to live outdoors so much and why I was staying on the beach now—because the real world *is* change, and here I was exposed to the elements with nothing to hide it.

Later that evening I wrote the following poem. It helped me digest the experience:

SKY-CHANGE

Once upon a time
there were no doors to shut
no walls to separate
we were always together
all of us—
the family together, the animals together—
and we watched
mother-change, father-change
child-change, and sky-change
all day.
Then we built houses
with doors and walls
and found ourselves alone in them
with pictures of one another,
pictures of sunsets and clouds,
and "sky-change" became "sky"
"mother-change" became "mother."
Now we live in two worlds
the changing one outside the walls
living, unpredictable, unknowable

and the frozen one inside
made up of word-pictures
thing-pictures, animal-pictures—
those mind-pictures we juggle so well.

Some time later when I encountered the Buddhist teachings on imper-manence, it was like meeting an old friend.

Now Is a Verb

Any attempt to get ahold of Now, to hold it, to think about it, to understand it, backfires. We make a thing out of it by intellectualizing it—but the "now" that we conceptualize is not the elusive Now in which we live.

Our life, a continuity of "Nows."

The Self Is a Verb, Too . . .

We try to make a thing out of the self also, and we identify with this thing that we make. Our identification may go something like:

I am my perceptions,
I am my states of mind,
I am my body . . .

Each of these statements may be true, but only for a moment, and only partially. In each case, it turns out that I am more. I am more than my thoughts. I am more than my states of mind.

When I identify with any part of me, I reduce the whole to a fragment of it. It is like saying, "I am my tooth." Now, it is true that when I have a toothache it does feel as if I am only this aching tooth, and only this pain. But there is more to me, and it is healing to see the larger picture. It is a consolation.

Mindfulness practice is keeping in mind that you are a verb that looks like a noun in the mirror. But it is also humoring that illusion without being taken in by it. Change is the reality, and permanence the illusion, although at first glance it may look as if the opposite is true.

Expecting permanence brings stress. Embracing change brings wisdom.

Driving Mindfully

"Before enlightenment, chop wood, carry water. After enlightenment, chop wood, carry water." This Zen saying focuses on two common activities of long ago as a Zen practitioner might do them before and after enlightenment. The activities themselves are the same, but now they are done wholeheartedly and with attention, without thinking of other things or carrying on unrelated discussions.

A theoretical understanding of mindfulness becomes applied mindfulness as we relate it to everyday activities, and today, driving is a more common activity for most of us than either chopping wood or carrying water.

The exercise below is not intended to transform you into a "Sunday driver," who drives annoyingly slowly, even "recklessly slow," as UrbanDictionary.com puts it.

The purpose is to put you in a good mood as you get on the road, to develop an awareness of the means as well as the ends, to counteract the propensity to be single-mindedly focused on destination, and to be aware of a tendency some of us have of slipping into competitive, angry, or impatient states of mind when we drive. Sing it slowly before you start (the melody is the familiar children's song "Row, Row, Row Your Boat"). I timed it: it only takes fifty seconds, and give yourself a bit of extra time to get where you are going—you may find it difficult to speed after singing this song!

Roll, roll, roll along, gently down the street,
Merrily, merrily, merrily, merrily, this drive is a treat.

Smiling as you go, happy and serene,

Merrily, merrily, merrily, merrily, life is but a dream.

Lightly like a kite, let your spirits lift,

Merrily, merrily, merrily, merrily, each day is a gift.

Comfy in your seat, as you make your way,

Merrily, merrily, merrily, merrily, have a pleasant day.

You might want to tape these words to your sun visor as a reminder.

11.

Change Your Story,
Change Your Identity

Why do you stay in prison
when the door is so wide open?

—RUMI

In "The Ugly Duckling," Hans Christian Andersen's popular children's story, a certain well-known bird turns from ugly to gorgeous in the blink of an eye. It succeeds in this feat without plastic surgery, a crash diet, or even a visit to the feather dresser. It does it by changing its story.

If "The Ugly Duckling" were a contemporary mainstream movie, it would be billed as a family drama, for it is the story of growing up in an unsupportive environment. The protagonist is different from her siblings and from other ducks around her, and suffers discrimination and cruel treatment. She becomes an unhappy loner, and at one point even considers suicide. When she sees other swans from a distance while still quite young, she gazes at them with a mix of admiration and envy, without realizing that she is beautiful like them. She has bought into the story of being ugly and unworthy, and is unable to shake it off, even when the truth winks at her from a distance.

She is lucky that she finally has her epiphany through circumstances: one day she accidentally finds herself in the company of other swans. Also accidentally, she sees her own reflection in the lake at the same time. Now she gets it. She assumes her new identity with gusto, in one stroke finding acceptance and company. We can assume that if the story were longer, we would also hear of her finding a romantic relationship and raising a family. We can also safely conclude that from now on, the label "ugly duckling" properly designates real ducklings in her mind, and does not include her.

This "seeing her reflection in the water" is an appropriate metaphor for seeing into one's true nature. At that moment, the young swan "found herself." Before, she had some wrong perceptions about herself. These wrong perceptions grew in her like weeds in a garden. First her family, then others around her watered the seeds of these wrong perceptions and helped them grow. Because of them, she could not be happy either by herself or with others. Her journey toward happiness started when she was able to see herself for who she was.

The eighteenth-century Scottish philosopher David Hume, like the Buddha twenty-two centuries before him, held that our sense of self consists of a bundle of experiences and perceptions. We do not directly experience the self. Instead, we experience sensations and perceptions. To this, the Buddha would add that we also experience our bodies, mental states, and a constantly shifting river of consciousness. We create our sense of self out of these. It follows that if our perceptions are erroneous, the sense of self we create out of them will be skewed. This is what happened to the young swan in the story. And the mental states of confusion and despair added to her bewilderment.

Before her insight, she showed signs of stress. Others bullied her, so she flew away and found somewhere to hide. Her sense of self and her true nature were in conflict, and she could find no peace. She felt that she was deficient, or not "good enough." A surprising number of people also report such feelings.

Imagine you are a bystander watching this lovely young swan and her drama, observing the bullying and her distress with a mixture of amazement and compassion, and you wonder: "Are you upset because you are not a duck?"

Her distress is a play in two acts: in Act One she is bullied by others. In Act Two she internalizes the bullies and bullies herself. I feel like that bystander when in the presence of human ugly ducklings suffering from stress—they are in Act Two of a strange play, bullying themselves. They are not even sure what their stress is all about anymore. They just want it to stop.

The first step in mindfulness is recognizing. Many people are unaware that they are telling themselves a tale. They have always seen themselves in a certain way. They have bought a story, and invested in it—the story is "them." You start to free yourself from your story when you begin to look deeply into your stress and see its roots. In the beginning this may be only a vague feeling. You have internalized the story so thoroughly that it has become unconscious. You don't articulate it in words, you just feel the stress.

We see clearly that, in this story, feelings of "not being good enough" were implanted in this bird during her upbringing. This may also be true for people who feel that way. They may have picked up and internalized certain stressful attitudes from their upbringing or culture. Please note, however, that these feelings are present *now*, and they must be faced *now*. Diving into one's past for clues is revealing and it brings insights about how we feel now, but it does not change the fact that we must still find ways of dealing with present feelings in the present moment.

Our attitude in examining the past is important—we can look at the past without going there, like we can open a door and look inside a room without going in. If a certain time in the past has been a torture chamber, we do not have to move back into the torture chamber. We can stay in the corridor of the present—just a peek through the door of the past is enough to bring understanding. Open the door, take a look, and move on. (Post-traumatic stress disorder involves *unprocessed* memories. Mindfulness can still help, but if you suffer from this disorder you need therapy as well.)

Recognize how you are feeding your stress now. Stress is like a fire—if you stop feeding it, it will soon go out. Think of the campfires you've enjoyed. You were constantly tending the fire, feeding it branches and logs to keep it going. The small branches were only good for a short while. Bigger branches and logs kept it going longer. What are those branches and logs that keep the fires of your stress going?

Here are five questions that can help you identify them:

1. What are the mental and physical habits that keep your stress going? How do you drive? Do you allow plenty of time to get to work? Do you allow yourself enough time with other obligations so that you are not always pressed for time?

2. What books, magazines, and Internet stuff do you read? What movies or programs do you watch? Do you participate in conversations that add to your stress? What kind of music keeps you company?

3. What kinds of automatic thoughts usually course through your mind? Do you identify with them or do you challenge them when they are anxious or stressful thoughts?

4. Is your attitude generally optimistic or pessimistic? How do you see the world and others? What is your level of trust and confidence?

5. Do you see yourself as part of the web of life, or do you see yourself separate from it?

Change Your Story, Change Your Attitude

If your story is a story of victimhood, consider that one can only be a victim of one's own thoughts.

Was Helen Keller a victim? She had a brain infection when she was nineteen months old that left her deaf and blind. Does that qualify one for victimhood?

Not in her case.

Once she learned to read Braille she progressed so fast that she attracted worldwide attention, even being invited to meet with President Calvin Coolidge. She passed the entrance exams for Radcliffe College (now integrated with Harvard University), even though the math portion of the exam used a different version of Braille with which she was not familiar. She found out about this two days before the exam, quickly mastered the new script, and aced her test.

Was Nelson Mandela a victim? Does being unjustly imprisoned for twenty-seven years qualify one for victimhood?

Not in his case.

Severe adversity did not destroy Mandela, Helen Keller, or Oprah Winfrey, who was raped at nine, became pregnant at fourteen, and lost her son in infancy. Does she look or act like a victim?

It would be simplistic to say that what happens to us does not matter. Of course it does. Yet the lives of these people and numerous others like them show that victimhood is an attitude of the mind more than the result of unfortunate circumstances. It is how we see ourselves, and how we spin our story. To reword a Buddhist saying, pain is inevitable, but victimhood is optional. As the Dalai Lama says in *The Wisdom of Compassion*:

"External circumstances are not what draw us into suffering. Suffering is caused and permitted by an untamed mind." So is stress. Self-pity, resentment, and avoidance not only create extra stress, they also absorb much of the energy that could be better used in moving forward.

Our Sense of Self

We usually link our sense of self with our story. Yet as we saw with the young swan as well as in the discussion of victimhood, our story is not necessarily a historically accurate narrative—it is based on our interpretation of events rather than on actual events. It can also be selective. We may be telling one story to our children and another to our sex therapist, for example (if we have a sex therapist). Marion Barry, the former mayor of Washington, D.C., did not originally include his use of crack cocaine in the story he told about himself to his constituents. Even when the intent is not to deceive, a story-based sense of self can be as fictional as the story it is based on. It can also cause us stress if we believe it.

An experience-based sense of self relates the self to the present moment rather than to the past. A fleeting bundle of sensations, perceptions, awareness, and mental states creates our sense of self. As Buddha said, the sense of self clings to us as a whole, and not only to our parts—it is "like a scent" that belongs to the whole flower, and not just to the stem or the petals.

"Self" is a noun. But it does not refer to a "thing"—self-realization is the progressive loss of a separate and thing-like sense of self. It is the loss of what we know as self, and the gaining of a self that is without boundaries.

This breathing, feeling thing that we are is part of the universe. This particular part of the universe is parceled out, and it has our name on it. It is like the side of a mountain that has been divided into lots for building condos. The lot with our name on it is not separate from the rest of the mountain, except in the mind. The bees and the plants do not see it as separate at all.

Each of us is a drop in the ocean of life. This drop does not have a box around it. It is not separate from the rest of the ocean. We swim in the ocean, and breathe the sky, our skin is porous like a sieve.

Our perceptions—are they entirely ours? If we have a perception of Nazis as cruel and racist, for example, is that perception entirely ours, or is it a collective perception of society?

Our consciousness, our mind—is it all ours? Our aggressiveness evolved as we fought to be the alpha male in a herd, our terror as we ran for cover as rabbits and crabs. Buddha's realization was that our evolutionary past still lives in us today. How else can we explain our anxieties, our murders, and our wars?

The self does not extend only through space, but through time as well.

The good news is that this extended self without boundaries encompasses not only animals and sea monsters, but also the Buddha and other enlightened beings. They are also part of the stream. The whole stream is present in each drop, and we are the stream now—we are its present. With mindfulness, we can own the enlightened side of our evolutionary heritage as well as its darker side.

◆

At the Bus Stop

Another guided meditation exercise. Here is a suggestion for this and the other guided meditation exercises: use the voice memo feature on your smartphone, iPod, or computer and record them. Read the lines slowly and pause for about twenty seconds between each instruction. This is a great way to make them your own, and to have them readily available for practice whenever you have some free time.

I'm sitting straight and tall

in touch with all the sensations of breath and of my posture.

I listen to the quality of the sensations coming from my feet and hands.

My hands touch each other. I listen to the sensations in my hands.

I listen to the sensations of sitting coming from my buttocks.

I listen to the sensations themselves.

My body does not speak English.

It does not speak in words, but in sensations.

I listen to the quality of the sensations coming from different parts of my body.

If words come to mind, I know that I'm not just listening,

but also interpreting and judging.

Now I just listen to the quality of the sensations.

If words come to mind, I dismiss them and continue listening.

I listen to the sensations of breath in the same way.

My in-breath and my out-breath feel a bit different.

I listen to the difference.

I visualize myself at the bus stop.

Each bus that comes to the stop is like a thought.

It wants to take me to another place.

I watch a bus come, the doors open, but I do not get on it.

I see different buses come and stop,

buses with different numbers indicating different destinations.

They open their doors, but I do not get on.

Breathing in and out, I stay present, I stay here.

Thoughts come and go like buses,

I just watch.

If I find myself on a bus because I lost my concentration, I get off.

I want to stay here, not go somewhere else where thoughts take me.

I stay with my breath

listening to all the sensations coming from my body.

I check for tensions in my body and mind.

Tensions can sneak up on me with the slightest loss of concentration.

Thoughts are the way my brain functions

just like breathing is the way my lungs work.

I keep the focus of my attention in my abdomen

where the breathing occurs.

12.

Relationships

I've arrived, I'm home here for thousands of years now
walking on the grass hand in hand with you
smelling the sweet air, hearing small birds sing
and finding peace in my heart.

—J. E.

I n his book *What Makes Love Last?* John Gottman estimates that close relationships add about a decade to our lives. Statistics concur—people in relationships live healthier lives and have fewer health problems. The benefits
do not end there. If we play our cards right and embrace our partner with
love and empathy, we gain access to another person's reality and get the
opportunity to see the world with a different pair of eyes, thus enriching
our vision and expanding our universe. I celebrated this feeling in a Valentine's Day poem for my partner, Suzanne:

The Himalayas are solid, heavy
and majestic, rising high above the plains
they know the wind and the snow

but they do not know the sea
do not know the play of the dolphin
the soft caress of the seaweed
or the colors of the slippery fish
that swim languorously through currents and tides
with glassy eyes.
They do not know the waves.
Without knowing you
I would be as ignorant as the mountains are of the sea
ignorant of half the world.
That half—
made of the same four elements as me
but woven so differently . . .

—J. E.

Different Realities

A man's reality can be different from a woman's—no doubt. There is more than one reality. And it doesn't end with Mars and Venus—senior citizens are from Jupiter, teenagers from Mercury, young boys from Neverland, and young girls from Wonderland. And our realities depend not only on age and gender, but also on culture, upbringing, and genes. Denying someone's reality, their feelings and perceptions, is stressful to them.

We get a sense of enrichment when we understand and appreciate each other's reality. If the world consisted only of seven billion Joseph Emets, it would be a much less interesting place, trust me. If we approach a dialogue with our partner in this spirit, it becomes a learning experience and brings us closer to the other. Understanding this intellectually, however, is different from putting it into practice. A mother can appreciate *Peter Pan* when she reads the book, but she can still be stressed when she is face-to-face with a real-life Peter Pan, as when her own boy acts like he is in Neverland.

How Do You See Your Partner?

One day, a change happened in my own perspective, as if I had suddenly stepped from my side of the gender fence over to my partner's, and I saw Suzanne in a new light.

I had felt like this once before when we first moved into our house and I stepped over a real fence to cross over to my new neighbor's yard. Until then, I had been looking at him and speaking to him from my side of the fence. When I crossed the fence that separated our yards and stood in the middle of his backyard, I noticed that it looked different. Not only that, but now my own backyard looked different.

Seeing my partner from her side of the fence I could also glimpse her story—she had lived in Wonderland as a young girl, and I could still feel traces of a certain Alice-like vibe when I looked at her now. I grew up in Neverland, a different place.

How do *you* see your partner—only from the perspective of your own needs, desires, and outlook, or do you feel that you penetrate his or her own reality and walk in his or her shoes? How would it *feel* to be your partner?

This thought experiment gives us a new willingness to validate and respect our partner's way of being. How does your partner see you? What does he or she want out of the relationship?

Love and Relationship

Love is a feeling.

Relationship is a story—it's the story of what we do with that feeling. It is love in action.

Classical poetry or religious texts do not talk much about relationships. They talk about love. "Love thy neighbor" sounds much better than "Have a relationship with thy neighbor."

"Relationship" is a relatively new word. The *Online Etymological Dictionary* says that it was first used in 1744, but only in the sense of kinship. It was first used to refer to romantic or sexual relationships in the 1940s, but this use must have been slow to catch on. My two-volume Oxford dictionary published in 1975 had not yet heard of it. Our parents and grandparents did not have relationships. They had affairs and marriages. Some of these affairs and marriages were also good relationships. Others were not.

Relationship Is a Two-Sided Coin

You can love somebody all by yourself, without the object of your love even knowing about it. But you cannot "relationship" alone. Love can be a one-sided coin. Relationship is more like a dance—it takes two. An invitation to dance is not yet a dance. The dance of relationship is moving harmoniously together through the bumps and grinds of each day while keeping time with the beat of love. Communication is part of its essence, but just like in a dance, this communication does not have to be verbal. A relationship is a kind of symbiosis that is beneficial to both partners. Therefore love, respect, and appreciation of each other's dissimilarities are also parts of its essence. *Romeo and Juliet* may be a good love story, but it is not a good relationship story. Those two did not live long enough to do the dance of everyday life together. And despite saying things like:

> *My bounty is as boundless as the sea,*
> *My love as deep; the more I give to thee,*
> *The more I have, for both are infinite . . .*

they were not beneficial to each other. In the end they destroyed each other.

Othello, another Shakespeare play, is even worse as a relationship story. Othello did not trust Desdemona, his beloved wife. Trust is the number one requisite for a good relationship, according to John Gottman. Othello was suspicious of his wife but did not share his feelings with her. In the end he strangled Desdemona out of jealousy. The feeling of love is a great beginning for a relationship. It is essential but not enough by itself. Other feelings, other skills are also important. Without them you have stressful or even destructive relationships.

A Relationship Is More Than Love

Contemporary poets no longer write as much love poetry as in Shakespeare's day. Educated suitors no longer compose love sonnets on the spot. We have learned to be a little wary of love. Love can be only mental or only emotional. It can be based on illusion or infatuation. A relationship has to involve more. In a relationship, the quality of everyday life is the poem. Perhaps our change of perspective has to do with the women's liberation movement. Now both partners are active agents in an equal sense. The two-sidedness of "relationship" is more in tune with the spirit of our time than the one-sidedness of "love." Women love just as passionately as men, but they have a strong focus on everyday life as well. They want to know what love means for the lover in practical terms, how emotion translates into behavior in a couple.

This emphasis on relationship is new. Ancient Greeks had a god and goddess of love, but not of relationships. Now Facebook is only interested in your relationship status. It does not care about your love status.

From Love to Relationship

Until recently, relationships between the sexes were orchestrated by nature to serve her own purpose of reproduction. Nature stacked the cards to fulfill her aims. But we have figured out how to get around her tricks and can now have relationships in order to serve our own purposes, and for the benefit of the relationship itself. A good relationship can be a growth experience as well as a refuge from the stresses of life. The following poem starts with love, and ends with relationship as a learning experience:

Through my love for you
I can feel the love in the Garden,
I can feel the love of all lovers
and now the meadows and hills,
and the river of nights and days
are wearing your face and smile.
Learning the art of love
I learn how to love the Earth,
I learn how to love every season,
I learn how to love each day,
with its sunshine, rain, or snow.
Each moment has its own spell.
Learning to live with you
I learn how to live with flowers,

I learn how to live with a song,
and I learn to live with my feelings:
my desire, my impatience, my dreams,
I learn to live with myself.
Learning the dance of love
is like learning to sail with the wind,
it's like learning to swim with the waves.
So I learn to dance with you,
by moonlight, sunshine, or clouds,
I learn to dance with change.

—J. E.

Are You Listening?

John Gottman has brought more than three thousand couples into his "Love Lab," an apartment near the University of Washington, where he has meticulously observed their interactions. He has found that couples pay full attention to each other's words only about 30 percent of the time. Based on this finding, he calculates that the likelihood that both partners will be listening to each other attentively at the same time is just 9 percent. No wonder there is so much miscommunication in the world! The ability to pay attention and to listen is an essential relationship skill, and also a cornerstone of the Buddhist path. This makes Buddhist practice particularly relevant in our time.

A Deity of Listening?

Buddhism may be unique among world religions in having a dedicated being in charge of listening. Though not a goddess in the traditional sense, the bodhisattva Quan Yin (also called Avalokiteshvara) is an archetypal presence who brings solace just by listening. Sometimes referred to as "the Female Buddha" in Chinese gift shops, she is an important figure in the lives of many Buddhists. There are often more people kneeling in front of her statue in a Mahayana temple than in front of the Buddha. Perhaps, for many of us, the need to open our hearts and be heard with attention and compassion is even more important than the thirst for wisdom. Partners in a relationship can satisfy this deep longing by listening wholeheartedly and actively to each other. Thich Nhat Hanh underlines this connection between being a Buddhist and practicing deep listening by articulating it explicitly as one of the Buddhist vows:

"Aware of the suffering caused by unmindful speech and the inability to listen to others, I vow to cultivate loving speech and deep listening."

If we could look into the bodhisattva Quan Yin's mind we may find thoughts like:

Just one drop, one single drop
of compassion is enough
to bring back spring on earth.

Like the Buddha, Quan Yin lives not in a statue but in our hearts. Listening wholeheartedly to our partner can be that drop of compassion that will bring back the freshness of spring into our relationship.

The Magic of Being Heard

On a personal level, expressing a feeling or a need allows you to own that feeling and that need, and you see things differently afterward. This is quite independent of any feedback you may receive from the listener. This is feedback you are receiving from *yourself* as you hear yourself speak. Expressing a feeling clarifies it for you. The listener acts as a midwife.

Being a Good Listener

In a way, listening is like meditation. It is allowing space for things to come to the surface and being there for them, except that now another mind has the floor. The same qualities that make you a good meditator, like being nonjudgmental and being open, also make you a good listener. Perhaps it is because of this similarity that listening is an integral part of Buddhist practice. This in turn makes Buddhism of interest to counselors and those seeking to improve their relationships.

There are certain temptations during listening. Interrupting the speaker is one of them. This happens when what you are hearing triggers a brilliant idea in your own mind that is clamoring to be heard. Turn your attention back toward the speaker when that happens. This time is about her, not about you.

If at any time you feel that some things still need clarifying for you or the speaker, you can become an active listener by asking pertinent questions.

Communication Habits

If you grew up with brothers and sisters, you may have learned to hold up your end in verbal exchanges. Often the aim in verbal tussles between young siblings is not to resolve disputes, but to somehow come out on top. In this kind of semiplayful verbal sparring, sarcasm is in—you defend yourself when attacked, and attack to win. This comes in handy in the jungle of the school yard as well, and the habit of talking to win points and to avoid losing them becomes entrenched. Watch out for this pattern if you or your partner has siblings who are close in age. It can be a very frustrating exercise if one partner is trying to express a need or attempting to be understood while the other is trying to score points or not lose them.

We develop other habits through games that do not work out well in communication. In Scrabble, you hide your hand. In card games, you hide your cards. You only play a card if it is going to win a point or get you an advantage. This is a poor strategy for heart-to-heart communication. If you make a habit of hiding your true motives or your true feelings, real communication goes out the window, and the conversation turns into another game.

Physical games leave a similar legacy. You play to win. I once played Ping-Pong with a monk in Plum Village. He was not trying to find my weak spots and score points the usual way. First I thought he was a beginner. But soon I revised my opinion. I noticed that he was returning all my fancy shots, but the ball always came back to the middle of my table at a convenient speed, and bounced to the same height. He was not using his skills to try to challenge me. It was a strange experience, and the wind went out of my sails. That monk had turned the tables by playing a competitive game cooperatively—cooperation had become his second nature, or rather, his first nature. He was probably playing Ping-Pong the way he communicated—compassionately and in a helpful way, while some of us communicate the way we play Ping-Pong—aggressively and to win. We listen and speak like lawyers in court.

Mindful Listening

In an address to members of the U.S. Congress, Thich Nhat Hanh offered this metaphor to describe how the healing energy of mindfulness works:

"When a baby cries, the mother stops everything she is doing and holds the baby tenderly in her arms. The energy of the mother will penetrate into the baby and the baby will feel relief. The same thing happens when we recognize and embrace our own pain and sorrow."

Ditto in a couple—the mindfulness energy of the listener penetrates into the heart of the speaker to alleviate her stress. This happens because mindfulness is a compassionate kind of energy like maternal kindness.

There is also mood contagion at play. We may not realize the effect of our mindfulness on others, but like other states of mind, mindfulness is contagious. Just *imagine* having a heated argument with the Buddha and you will see what I mean! It would be hard to get worked up in the presence of somebody who listens with calm and compassionate attention.

When listening to our partner, we can listen not just to the words we hear, but also to the voice behind the words—not just to the explicit meanings of the words, but also to the longing behind the words. It is this willingness and determination to go beneath the surface that takes whole-hearted concentration. People communicate on many levels at once, with body language and emotions as well as with words. In order to hear our partner on all those levels, we need to listen on many levels also—with the heart as well as with the mind, and with the whole mind instead of with just a part of the mind.

"Listening stitches the world together," writes Mark Nepo in his book *Seven Thousand Ways to Listen*. It also stitches our body together as our cells and organs listen to one another's chemical and electrical messages, and it stitches a couple together as they listen to the overt and covert messages coming from each other.

A Refuge from Stress

Women and men are fundamentally different and fundamentally alike. Some of our differences are obvious, but many others are invisible. Each cell in a woman's body is different from each cell in a man's: it has an extra X chromosome instead of an X and a Y. Our brains have subtle differences in form and function, and our hormones are different. We are more different than we often realize, and we are also more alike.

Our natures are at the same time complementary, similar, and conflicting—we need each other, yet we also have opposing needs. We can be happy or unhappy together—a situation tailor-made for stress as well as for happiness: Which is it going to be?

> *The Earth is a garden of love, and a house of mirrors*
> *where love and needs are mixed together.*
> *Here women and men live under the same sun*
> *dreaming with their eyes open, and loving with their eyes closed.*
> *They are similar and different from head to toe*
> *together and in love, or apart and out of love.*
> *Sometimes they pretend to be angels or demons*
> *sometimes they are a refuge for each other.*
>
> —J. E.

The Way of Mindfulness

"When another person makes you suffer, it is because he suffers deeply within himself, and his suffering is spilling over. He does not need punishment; he needs help." Whether our partner's stress is spilling over in the form of anger, accusations, grouchiness, or complaints, we can keep Thich Nhat Hanh's words in mind and respond with kindness: "Is something bothering you? Can I help?"

We can respond like the Ping-Pong–playing monk who returned my aggressive moves with gentleness. This requires us to tame our own automatic reactions. If we respond with anger, we create more stress, and we are off to another round of aggressive Ping-Pong.

Our mindfulness has a positive effect on the well-being of the other people in our life. Mindfulness practice trains us to become aware of our breathing and our bodily reactions and to monitor them. With this awareness we can avoid reacting emotionally. We are able to respond thoughtfully—in a way that takes the needs of others into consideration. We avoid creating more stress all around.

Happiness

Good relationships make us happy, and happiness makes good relationships possible. If there is a secret to tackling this chicken-and-egg situation head-on and advancing both our happiness and our relationships at the same time, it would have to be positivity—the habit of seeing and appreciating the healing ointment rather than the proverbial fly in the ointment, and the willingness to express our appreciation to others. And behind what we say, there has to be what we feel—otherwise our words would be just empty and unconvincing compliments.

Psychologists suggest making up to five positive comments for each critical comment you make to someone whose relationship you value. To be on the safe side, you can be as generous as possible with positive comments. Be aware that too many critical comments can damage a relationship, especially if they become a habit. Above all, do not imitate the tax auditor that Shawn Achor writes about in his book *The Happiness Advantage*. This man created an Excel spreadsheet listing all the mistakes his wife had made over a period of six weeks, and presented it to her. Perhaps he thought this would improve their relationship. I'm sure you can guess that it didn't—she divorced him soon after that.

Our professional training may increase our bias for seeing what's wrong rather than what's right. Achor considers that accountants cultivate this bias every day, because so much of their work consists of finding mistakes and spotting errors in tax returns. But you do not have to be a tax accountant to have a critical attitude. We all have it to some degree, and it can come in handy when used appropriately. I'm using it now to spot errors and inaccuracies in this manuscript as I go over it with a picky eye. The problem comes when this becomes a runaway habit and our default way of relating to people and to circumstances. Then it becomes toxic. And not only for relationships. I'm reminded of an encounter in San Pedro on the shores of Lake Atitlán in the Guatemalan highlands. This indigenous village is built around charming grassy foot trails instead of roads, and the day before I had discovered that there is a species of butterfly that lands on the lake and floats. I had spent a dreamy afternoon in a kayak surrounded by floating butterflies and watching puffs of smoke from a live volcano. Then I had supper with a couple from New York whose conversation was mostly about the shortcomings of their bathroom and the poor quality of the toilet paper.

It takes mindfulness to hear the voice of the inner critic without fusing with it and *becoming* it. And it takes practice to cultivate the precious skills of valuing and appreciating.

If you have children, you can do it as a family at the dining table, each person mentioning three good things that happened to them during the day. This would have the added benefit of channeling the conversation in a positive direction. You can think about it at bedtime as a sort of evening prayer, or you can write about it in a diary. You can be more specific and write down three things you appreciate most in your partner. Or you can do it another way and write about what you would miss most if your partner weren't there. Even more specific is what you would have missed *today* without your partner—each day has its own joys and blessings. As your attitude becomes more appreciative, your words and acts of appreciation become more heartfelt, and they are valued more.

✦

Autumn Leaves

Here's another guided meditation exercise. Sit up straight in the meditation posture and avoid slouching or lying down. Good posture is part of your body language—it's how you speak to yourself and to others without using words. Here's a suggestion: take one slow breath between instructions as you read the text. This may prove to be a much-needed "patience exercise" to ground you in the present moment.

I take three deep and slow breaths,

concentrating on the physical sensations of breathing.

I slowly become aware that there are thoughts lingering in my mind.

The thoughts in my mind are surface thoughts

like the autumn leaves that blow in the wind.

They go round and round.

They are left over from a time past, a time now gone.

Like autumn leaves are left over from summer and spring.

Those leaves were right for their time, for spring and summer.

but now they are relics.

They are no longer attached to trees.

My thoughts about the past are also relics.

They are not attached to reality anymore.

They just keep blowing around on the surface of my mind.

I shift my attention away from the blowing leaves.

I shift my attention to my breathing.

I concentrate on my breath for five cycles.

Each cycle consists of an in-breath, a slight pause, an out-breath, and a longer pause.

Now I give myself a challenge:

How many breathing cycles can I fully stay with without getting lost in thought?

I count each cycle by curling a finger.

I repeat the challenge to see if I can stay longer with my breathing.

I go deeper, riding on my breath.

I leave behind the blowing leaves

and listen to the quiet space inside me.

As my breath becomes deeper and slower, I go deeper into myself, and I listen.

It is like going deep into the Earth.

I am just breathing and listening.

There is a quiet space within, under the noise of the blowing leaves.

I listen to my body. Is there tension somewhere?

In my face muscles, shoulders, legs, abdomen, or anywhere else?

I listen to my breath. Is it deep and slow, or short and shallow?

Is it rhythmic and regular?

I listen to my feelings. What am I feeling now? What is my internal weather like?

Is my internal weather sunny or cloudy, foggy or clear? Is it warm or cold?

If I become aware of the autumn leaves stirring again,

I listen deeper to see what wind stirs these leaves. They look alive in the wind.

It's the wind that makes them look alive.

I turn my gaze away from the leaves, to the blue sky above.

The sky is deep and vast.

I listen to my breath,

and I feel a deep peace within.

13.

Our Illusions and Our Burdens

Each moment is a chance to make peace with the world.

—THICH NHAT HANH

Atlas is a deity who carries the world on his shoulders in Greek mythology. He is often portrayed as a powerful man in his prime, a match for his task. But he is also sometimes shown as an older man bending under the weight he carries.

When I first encountered the world of Greek mythology in a college class, I did not relate these mythic deities to my inner world, at least not consciously. It was only later that I began to suspect that Apollo, Eros, Narcissus, and, yes, Atlas represent aspects of myself.

We carry our world on our shoulders because it is a world of our making. We are carrying "our" world. This world is as heavy or as light as we think it is.

The Burdens of Our Illusions

Living with illusions can be stressful—it can be a burden.

Mourning one's illusions can also be stressful, at least for a time.

Maggie came to see me and quickly burst into tears. Sometimes just talking about a disappointment opens a wound and makes it bleed again. She was not happy at home. Her husband found it impossible to express any feelings, but had no difficulty in constantly dumping all his work-related frustrations on her. He also had trouble relating to their teenage son and was in constant conflict with him. For all she could see, their son was a normal young boy "being himself." But her husband could not handle his son's "normal" behavior and constantly blew his lid when he spoke with him.

Our second meeting also had a short, tearful episode, but this time Maggie got over her distress faster. During subsequent meetings she developed a "Plan B." She was finding that her life at home had become a draining experience—she was not getting any nourishment out of it. She made detailed arrangements for moving out, and moving in with a friend, "just in case," but did not take the step.

Maggie did not cry during the third meeting. Subsequently, she began to cheer up. By our sixth meeting we were often laughing together. She was still living with the same man, who still had the same habits, but somehow she had found peace instead of frustration and anger inside herself. When I asked her what had changed, she used the metaphor of driving a car: "I am like a little car now—I'm not bothered by the other cars and trucks on the road. I make my own journey. I am not disturbed by whatever they do." Several times she described with her hands a car making a winding journey through the air. She was smiling with contentment.

Maggie had mourned her cherished illusions about her husband, and her grief at the loss of her illusions had finally run its course. I could not help noticing that she experienced this loss like any other loss—with tears at first, then with serenity, and finally she found her old joie de vivre again. She had learned to take her own feelings and "poor me" thoughts with a grain of salt, and to observe them with some detachment. And she had learned to focus on what was right with her husband instead of what was wrong with him. It turned out that there were many good things about him that she appreciated. He was a creative entrepreneur and had a good sense of humor—he contributed cartoons to the local weekly.

Maggie stopped seeing her world through her dreams. She gradually learned to give up her expectations of an ideal life with an ideal partner and accept things as they are. When the picture of an ideal is very strong in us, we compare what actually exists with that ideal and see actual people as deficient. If real people do not fit our ideal images, we may continue to hope that one day they will change. The crisis comes when we begin to realize that this is not happening, and is not likely to happen. Another curious thing—we tend to see the people who come up short of our ideals as lacking in moral fiber, as somehow morally deficient. Without realizing it, we have set ourselves up as an arbiter in moral matters. Even worse, we may take their quirks and idiosyncrasies personally—as if they were done on purpose to irritate us.

At that moment we face a difficult choice—either give up the ideal or give up the "imperfect" life and the "imperfect" people we share it with. Sometimes, as when violence is involved, the choice is obvious. At other times, as in Maggie's case, it may come to a toss-up, as she prepared the ground for a separation but did not take the actual step. It's surprising how having a "Plan B" ready to go can help clarify our thoughts.

Most of the time some measure of acceptance is called for—our rigid ideals only serve to make us stressed. Our vision of an ideal life with ideal people may be a burden, and letting go of it may bring freedom.

Carrying Our Burdens

I enjoy finding new meaning in old songs. The gospel/spiritual sometimes known as "Down by the Riverside" and sometimes as "Gonna Lay Down My Burden" is one of these:

Gonna lay down my burden,
   Down by the riverside . . .

I imagine slaves carrying bundles of their masters' laundry down to the river to wash. I imagine a sunny afternoon, and people making their way to the riverside through a winding path. There, they meet others like them. I imagine that this is a nice break from their usual kind of drudgery in the cotton fields, and the pressure is momentarily off. Perhaps they gossip and laugh, perhaps they sing and dance for a while. The burden they lay down is the physical burden of the bundles they carry. But the mental burden of always having someone on their backs is also laid down for now.

Perfectionistic expectations can also be burdens. They can prevent us from being happy as we are, with what we have. We cling to our expectations, we identify with them, and we do not want to give them up. It may take a crisis to force us to reevaluate the situation and make this difficult choice.

Appropriately, another verse from this spiritual goes:

I ain't gonna study war no more,
   study war no more . . .

When we lay down our illusions, we are on the way to peace. When we cling to our image of ideal people and ideal situations, we are at war with reality. If our high expectations are about ourselves, we are at war with ourselves. If our expectations are about others, we are at war with them. When a crisis comes, we have to give up something—either we have to give up our ideals and high expectations, or we have to give up the people who do not live up to them. Whatever we give up is initially experienced as a loss, and we grieve. But, as Maggie did, after a while we can also experience this "giving up" as a relief.

This is a growth process. We have gained new wisdom, and we live with more freedom in our hearts. We see people as they are, instead of through the lens of our expectations. It is a liberating experience, and it allowed

Maggie to rediscover her smile and her joie de vivre. On the other hand, clinging to ideals as well as the people who fall short of them is a depressing experience. The grief never ends, the disappointments never stop. We are not willing to give up either our expectations or the people who irritate us with their shortcomings.

When that happens we get mired in stress, for this is not a suffering that leads to enlightenment—it is a never-ending grief that skirts clear of enlightenment. We are resisting growth. This is a spiritual problem that cannot be solved by pharmacological means—it can be solved by gently pointing the sufferer toward acceptance. Acceptance is a third alternative between rejection and capitulation, when neither of these is acceptable. Acceptance does not mean capitulation, because it also implies finding our own boundaries—allowing others to be who they are does not mean that we have to live *their* life. We also accept ourselves as we are while we accept others as they are. At the same time that we recognize others' freedom, we allow ourselves the same measure of freedom.

You liberate others at the same time that you liberate yourself.

Carry Your Burdens Lightly

The story of the Chinese monk Hotei provides another twist on the metaphor of the burden. Hotei was an eccentric wanderer who lived during the tenth century. He is the "fat Buddha" who we often encounter in Chinatown or in Chinese restaurants. To many people who only know this laughing character, he is *the* Buddha, although in reality some sixteen centuries separate the two. Buddha and Hotei are also separated by their ethnic origin—Buddha is Indian and Hotei, Chinese. There are other differences—Buddha is tall and slender, Hotei short and fat. Buddha smiles, Hotei laughs.

Hotei lived during the flowering of Zen in China, and is featured in a Zen koan. He used to travel from village to village carrying a sack on his back—his "burden." Tradition has it that his bag was full of treats and toys for children. He was a kind person. But considering that he was constantly on the go, I think that it must have contained a good measure of dirty laundry as well, thus linking him, at least in my mind, to the slaves who walked down to the riverside with similar burdens on their backs.

One day a Zen monk went up to him and asked, "What is the meaning of Zen?"

Hotei put his bag down.

"How does one realize Zen?" the Zen monk asked again.

Hotei then picked up his bag and continued on his way.

This koan also illustrates dropping one's burdens, but goes further. We all have responsibilities in this world—responsibilities toward children, parents, partners, and work. An enlightened life is not one of shirking these responsibilities, but having a different attitude toward them. Mother Teresa had much to do, caring for many needy people each day. I do not think that she considered this a burden. She "shouldered" these responsibilities willingly, as Hotei did in the second part of the koan. I cannot imagine her complaining with a sour face about how much work she had to do. She could easily replace Hotei in this story.

Our burdens feel lighter if we carry them out of love instead of as an obligation. When obligation is replaced by generosity, choice enters into the equation, and with choice comes willingness instead of a sense of enslavement. The slaves did not have the freedom of choice, so they picked up their burdens with the same sense of obligation as before. But perhaps they picked them up a little more lightheartedly after that sunny afternoon by the river.

This spirit of willingness is in evidence in volunteer work. By definition, a volunteer is doing what he does willingly—he chooses to do it. What we do for others can be done willingly and out of generosity. The other side of the coin, of course, is knowing our limits. Hotei was wise—he did not try to carry a sack that was too heavy for him. Otherwise he might have hurt his back, and might not even have been able to walk anymore.

✦

Turning Burdens into Flowers

What burdens are you carrying?

The purpose of this exercise is first to identify your "burdens," and then to learn to carry them lightly, like Hotei in the Zen story.

Reread the two stories of the southern slaves and of Hotei on pages 176–180. Then make a list of everything that you see as an obligation in your life—work, care of children, looking after aging parents, the house, shopping for food, and food preparation—the whole enchilada. If you do many things out of a sense of obligation, your list can be long!

Next, practice dropping all your obligations for a moment and see what that feels like. This is the stage where the slaves laid down their burdens and Hotei put down his bundle. This stage is temporary—for you, it could be taking a walk in the park. Leave yourself lots of space to let off pressure and savor the feeling of freedom. Do not even think of your usual responsibilities for the time being. Drop them mentally as well as physically.

Now embrace your activities out of love and generosity instead of a sense of obligation. With willingness instead of resentment. Embrace the activities, but not the stress that used to accompany them. Burdens feel lighter that way. Recast your job as one of bringing a smile and some joy to the working day of your coworkers or clients. Start with yourself. Remember: Hotei is laughing. No forced gaiety is called for, however. Just be yourself, with a dose of kindness and a willingness to treat everybody like you would like to be treated yourself.

With your children or partner, remind yourself that you do what you do for them willingly and out of love. Like offering them flowers. Let everything you do be a flower offering.

14.
Work and Stress

Choose a job you love, and you will never have to work a day in your life.
—CONFUCIUS

Retire from Stress, Not from Work

At the first session of a Mindfulness Training for Stress Reduction class, I often ask participants to tell the group about the main cause of stress in their lives. In one group, Mark, a retired audiologist, spoke first: "I was so happy when I was still working. I had my own office, and I also did some work for the Institute for the Blind. It was rewarding to be of help to people who needed my services. Now I feel pretty useless. I have the whole day in front of me with nothing to do. It is very stressful."

Next to him sat Melinda, a thirty-six-year-old lawyer with two young children. Her story of stress was quite different: "I'm so busy. I have to prepare cases, schedule court appearances, answer questions on the phone. Then I come home, and the girls want a piece of me. It is very stressful not to have any downtime."

Mark and Melinda gave each other a puzzled look—they seemed to be living on different planets. But are they really?

The Treadmill and the Cliff

Sometimes, the world of work looks like it is organized purposefully to create extra stress. Just when many of us are working hardest to promote our careers, children come. Soon after, ailing parents may also demand our attention. In an article titled "Life on Overload: 'Sandwich Generation' Struggles with Burnout," *Globe and Mail* reporter Tavia Grant writes: "More working Canadians are having to care for both their children and elderly relatives, a squeeze that is triggering higher absenteeism, stress, and increasing burnout." There also may be workplace pressure to put in extra hours—while the workweek is lightening in some countries like the Netherlands, where it is twenty-seven hours, and France, where it is thirty hours, it is lengthening beyond the traditional forty hours in the United States. Even when employers do not overtly demand long hours, workers often put them in because they think they will have a better shot at promotions that way. Other workers just get "caught up" in a workplace ethic that values "passionate commitment." Melinda was living through this dizzying period in her life.

A long workday creates extra stress. This takes a toll on many fronts. Here is one of them: according to the National Cancer Institute, evidence from experimental studies suggests that psychological stress can affect a tumor's ability to grow and spread.

Then, suddenly, all this busyness will end, and at some point Melinda's life will begin to look like Mark's—children will grow up and leave home, retirement will come, and aging parents will move to a group home or pass away. The erstwhile busy person may now feel like she just fell off a cliff. From the stress of being too busy, she has gone to the stress of not having enough to do. And from dreaming about retirement, she may now shift to yearning for some meaningful occupation to fill her empty days.

Mindful Transitioning

After his retirement as a math professor at Université du Québec, Eugene, whom I have had the pleasure of knowing personally, never looked back. He tutored high school students in math as a volunteer three days a week well into his nineties. He was particularly good at helping the kind of student who has mathphobia. His in-depth knowledge of the subject and good humor made it possible for him to present math in a nontraditional way. You can probably think of examples of people in your own community who have successfully transitioned into meaningful retirement. Such people have met the following challenges:

- While they were working, purpose and meaning were provided by their workplace. Now they have to find those in their own hearts.

- Discipline was provided by the hours and the demands of the workplace. Now they have to find discipline in themselves.

- The obligation to earn a living and to provide for their family kept them going while working. Now they have to find compelling reasons within themselves.

Some amount of stress is built into the structure of our working life. If we are aware of some of the traps of the world of work, we can be better prepared to deal with them. The following paragraph recounts a strategy I have found immensely useful.

Can You Rest While Working?

Some time ago, Thich Nhat Hanh announced that he was going to China on a three-week teaching tour, and he invited people who were in his practice community to come along. I jumped at the chance and signed up. But when I saw the proposed schedule, I started to have second thoughts. Each day was full of activities from morning until evening. No time for rest. I doubted my ability to survive and enjoy this trip, and went to discuss my concerns with Sister Annabel Laity, one of the organizers. She listened, and looked over the schedule I had put before her. Then she said something I have never forgotten: "Why don't you rest during the activities?" I looked up and saw a relaxed woman. Was she at work now, as part of the organizing team for this complicated tour taking us through ancient mountaintop temples and answering all manner of questions from the three hundred or so participants, or was she resting? I saw that she was indeed doing both—she was practicing what she had asked me to do.

Resting while working is indeed possible with mindfulness. But I'm going to go one step further and suggest that, without mindfulness, rest is not readily available even when you make a special time for it. Even when you separate your work and rest periods, you may not be able to rest during the time you set out as your rest break. Why? Because your mind might still be going, worrying about something or other, or fussing about something that happened yesterday that you find upsetting. Your mind may be reliving that upset over and over again and flooding your body with the same stress hormones that it produced during the actual event.

Indeed, the ability to truly rest is one of the benefits of being in the moment. To many people this is not obvious. They may say, "If I want to rest, I just lie on the couch." Yet if the mind is not in the moment, it will not be on the couch with you. It will be somewhere else, and not at rest. And when the mind is not at rest, the body will not be at rest either. Mind and body are not separate. You can review the practice section of chapter 10, "Driving Meditation," and apply the insights presented to work, or even to lying on the couch. When lying on the couch, just lie on the couch. When working, just work—without resentment, worry, or overthinking. Work with your mind at peace and a smile in your heart. Do not get caught up in other people's stress and panic. This will be within your reach if you do the exercises in this book as indicated.

The fact is, by retiring from work, you do not necessarily retire from stress, and to retire from stress, you do not necessarily have to retire from work.

Working When You Do Not Need the Money

Mark didn't need the money, but he needed the engagement work provides. Humans evolved to be active—to walk, to run, to gather, to garden, and to hunt. They did not evolve to drive to the grocery store, use the washing machine, or order takeout. Every day that we are not physically active sets us back in our quest for good health and longevity; every day that we are not following a dream brings us closer to the dust heap. And it is not as if there are no dreams worth pursuing. The need to work for a better world, and the need to work for a more peaceful and just society are there as urgently as they have ever been. As Mark discovered, a life without work isn't what he thought it would be—a time of freedom and fun. He may have looked forward to retirement, sometimes counting the days, but when it came, it came together with a loss of purpose and a loss of his accustomed place in life.

Living contrary to our true nature brings stress. The following poem was written while watching pelicans on the seashore in Mexico on a vacation:

Many hours of flying, soaring, and diving each day
in order to eat that day.

No way to separate eating from flying
the beak from the wings—
pelicans would not understand
"Give us this day our daily fish."
We have taken that prayer literally
we wait for someone to give us our food
we wait at the grocery store
we wait at the restaurant
and some of us even wait at home
slowly dying with each meal
from not flying.

—J. E.

Were these pelicans working, or at leisure? Do they know the difference?

No Work, No Food

Pai Chang (720–814) was a Chinese Zen master who was assiduous about working every day, and continued his daily routine of work even when he was very old. Out of concern for his well-being, some of the monks urged him to take it easy, and to rest. When he wouldn't, they hid his gardening tools. Pai Chang then refused to eat. He said, "A day of no work is a day of no eating."

We may feel admiration for his noble gesture, and no doubt it was an admirable gesture. But Pai Chang perhaps had another, more down-to-earth motive as well—he may not have wanted to experience the feeling of uselessness and the stress of boredom that sometimes comes with retirement.

Pai Chang was living like the pelicans. He was also working like the pelicans—his work activities of gardening and teaching were directly related to his life. Like the pelicans, if his leisure time looked like work, his work also looked like leisure.

Unremitting leisure without a trace of usefulness to others or to the world and work done unwillingly may both feel stressful.

Light a Small Candle

Lighting a small candle and cursing the darkness both start the same way—by becoming aware of a problem or a need that is not being properly addressed. But then, they part ways. Cursing the darkness may give us a feeling of superiority—we know better than those people who are stuck in darkness, we are better than they. But our cursing is not helping anyone. It is an act of criticism.

Lighting a small candle is an act of love.

Many years ago, I read a story about a woman who at her death finds herself being irresistibly pulled toward heaven with a carrot in her hand. At first she is surprised and puzzled. Then she begins to remember—as a young girl she had passed by a homeless man in the street. On the spur of the moment, she reached into the lunch bag her mother had prepared for her and pulled out a carrot to give to the homeless man. Now, on the strength of that one act of kindness, she was going to heaven.

Here's the practice: keep this story in mind, and be ready.

The image of Green Tara, a Tibetan meditation deity, exemplifies this attitude of readiness. Green Tara sits in the meditation posture—but only one leg is pulled back the usual way. The other is forward a bit, so she is ready to leap up and help when she's needed. Is someone being denied access to a bus because she doesn't have money? If you are ready like the Green Tara, you will recognize the opportunity.

There are many ways of lighting a small candle. Valerie, who lives on the ground floor of a duplex in a residential area of Montreal, dreamed up an interesting project.

She built a small red house with a sliding glass front window and space for about thirty books in it, and placed it on the fence in front of her lawn. It has a sign that reads: "Bring a book, take a book." She reports that it has become a busy place.

You might wonder how lighting a small candle relieves stress. Cursing the darkness drains you. You relive the same emotions of irritation and anger each time you rant and rave. In contrast, lighting a small candle nourishes your soul. When you get involved in an activity that is close to your heart, you can feel your stress fading away.

Whatever else you do, however, just be prepared to share some carrots: you never know.

15.

Finding Balance
with a Spiritual Path

We are born as flowers.

—THICH NHAT HANH

In the Flower Garland sutra, the Buddha describes the universe as one single flower. The Earth is a flower, and each being on Earth is also a flower.

This view contrasts sharply with the business view of people as "labor." Many businesses tend to treat people as cogs in a machine. Indeed, some treat machines better than people, because machines are costly investments.

Businesses may have difficulty with a workforce made up of flowers.

But humans experience stress when they are seen and treated without consideration and respect—respect not only for our rights but also for our nature. We have both our flower nature and the ability to work effectively inside us. We are both "labor" and "flower." It is clear that a balance is needed between these two ways of looking at humans, of looking at ourselves. We must first find that balance within. When we find it inside, it will be easier to search for it outside.

Spiritual paths have endured through the centuries for a reason—they are vehicles for important insights about life. Some of these insights are lost or are not sufficiently articulated in our individualistic, utilitarian worldview. Land is money, time is money, and "human resources" are also money. Reducing everything to money creates stress, because it makes for meaningless days and nights, and also because deep inside we know that there is more to life than money. Thich Nhat Hanh articulates this deep knowledge in a poem:

> *Each moment you are alive is a gem,*
> *shining through and containing earth and sky,*
> *water and clouds.*

In Thich Nhat Hanh's holistic universe, there is no wall between the apparent nonmaterial nature of time and the apparent materiality of the Earth.

In a footnote to another poem ("Cuckoo Telephone"), Thich Nhat Hanh elaborates further: "A friend who visits you without some moonlight in his or her traveling bag is too busy. When you see such a friend, ask him or her, 'Do you have enough moonlight in your bag?' That would be a bell of mindfulness."

Do you have enough moonlight in your bag?

"Do not think of heaven and earth as this world or the next; know that they coexist eternally in each passing moment," said Dōgen, the thirteenth-century founder of the Sōtō school of Zen. Let us find a way to live in these coexisting worlds simultaneously.

"Each flower, each leaf is a letter from the land of interbeing," Thich Nhat Hanh adds. "Interbeing" is his word for the web of all beings. As we cherish these letters and read them over and over, we slowly earn our place in that web as well.

A spiritual path can contribute to expanding our notion of love beyond romantic love. It points the way toward another aspect of love that is free of possessiveness, self-centeredness, and exclusiveness. It opens our eyes to compassion, empathy, and loving-kindness, which is a friendly kind of feeling, a wish for all persons to find happiness. This, in turn, improves our relationships—even romantic relationships can benefit from an expansion of the notion of love that comes from spiritual practice.

Not least, a spiritual path brings solace in the face of death. Buddhism does not even believe that you and I really exist as separate beings, except in a conventional sense. The photos in our fashion magazines and tabloids confirm our prevailing notion that the bodies in the pictures *are* those people. When we look in the bathroom mirror, we think, "This is me." Buddhists acknowledge that, while there is some truth to this (the image is definitely not of someone else), it is more accurate to identify with our actions. Our body is always changing—I have a photo of one of my daughters in a salad bowl as a newborn. She has changed quite a bit since then. One day, my own body will change even more radically and be recycled by nature. Our actions, however, echo through centuries. Martin Luther King Jr. is still alive today if we think of him in terms of his actions. If we think of him in terms of his body, he has been dead for a long time.

Identifying with one's body can understandably bring anxiety in the face of death.

Identifying with one's actions can bring solace. "Love is never lost," as Margaret says in Mitch Albom's novel *The Five People You Meet in Heaven*. This is also the message of the following poem:

I do not see the moon from my window tonight
but I see the milky sky
luminous like the early dawn
and the forest that was gold yesterday afternoon is
waving silvery leaves in its glow.
This light, suffusing all is
the moon without the moon.
There are other moons
that I do not see from my window—
parents, teachers, discoverers
and mother bears in the forests
all those who ever held
a young one to their bosom, and her hand in their own
and have always known

that kindness travels through generations
it is their light
that makes this world bright.

—J. E.

The relation between stress and illness is a chicken-and-egg situation—stress is a contributing factor in many illnesses, and illness in turn adds to our stress. And the fear of death is a huge stressor as well. However, death is death, it is what it is. It is the emotions and thoughts around it that can be very stressful.

Close your eyes for a moment and concentrate on the stream of sensations that passes for our sense of self. Death is simply the end of that stream. The end of the reel, the end of the movie. And then silence. In itself, that is not the hugely frightening experience that we make of it. We contribute to making death into a stressful monster with our thoughts and feelings around it.

We are programmed by evolution to fight for our life, and the metaphor of battle—battling an illness, for example—shapes our feelings. Then, death means that we have lost the battle. But is life really a battle to win or lose? If losing this battle means death, what then would winning it mean? Living forever? The battle metaphor makes us all feel like losers in the end. Why not see life as a gift? If you receive a gift of $10,000 someday, would that not also be enjoyed and spent? Can you enjoy $10,000 without spending it or using it in some way?

Stressful Life Passages

I once heard a radio interview with the Canadian dancer Margie Gillis. She said that it is not only children who have growth spurts. She said she had recently experienced a growth spurt of sorts, and within a period of six months grew from a young woman into a middle-aged one.

Change sometimes sneaks up on us, making us think that it happened suddenly when in fact it never stops happening. On a certain day, we realize it is summer. At a certain moment we realize it is night. We may realize one day that the kind of relationship we had with our son or daughter has a "best before" date that is fast approaching. During life passages, we are between two identities, and we may still cling to our former one even when we see the writing on the wall. This clinging creates stress. One day the young woman moves out of that box and into the "middle-aged woman" box. She has, in fact, been moving in that direction every day. But that particular day it hits her with full force. This experience is a sort of midlife crisis. Stress arises when we do not realize that all our definitions of self are temporary.

Taking our situational and temporary identities too seriously creates stress.

We can embrace our passing identities with enthusiasm provided that we remain true to who we are at our core, and a spiritual path makes this easier. It makes it possible to assume our responsibilities wholeheartedly while keeping a tongue-in-cheek attitude at the same time.

A story from the life of the eighteenth-century Japanese Zen master Hakuin illustrates this attitude well:

An unmarried girl who lived near Hakuin's temple became pregnant. Her angry parents demanded to know who the father was. The girl wanted to protect her lover, and in her panic she named Hakuin.

When the baby was born, the parents took it to him. They told him that he should take care of the baby because he had seduced their daughter.

"Is that so?" said Hakuin. He took the baby and lovingly and whole-heartedly took care of it for several months or years—accounts differ. Then, the real boyfriend showed up and confessed. He now wanted to marry the girl. The girl's embarrassed parents went to see Master Hakuin again and told him with many apologies that he should give the baby back to them because he was not the father.

"Is that so?" said Hakuin, as he handed back the baby with a smile.

The story brings to life the saying "When life hands you a lemon, make lemonade."

It also brings balance, equanimity, and compassion to an emotionally charged subject.

◆

Walking Meditation

Walk and touch peace every moment.
Walk and touch happiness every moment.
Each step brings a fresh breeze.
—THICH NHAT HANH

Many beginning meditators remark that when they sit in meditation, they notice that their minds are full of thoughts. Indeed, the mind is full of thoughts most of the time—we become aware of this when we sit in meditation, because we don't have something like a book or conversation to distract us.

When we walk, we take this busy mind with us. Even in paradise.

Wa'ahila Ridge State Park in Oahu, Hawaii, comes as close to paradise as you will get this side of heaven. I had gone there to explore the interior of the island after a Zen retreat at the Diamond Sangha at the beginning of my Buddhist journey. At first the pleasure of getting out of the car, breathing the air heavy with the scent of pine trees, and finding myself in the quiet of the woods got all my attention. But a half hour into the hike, the novelty had worn off, and I suddenly noticed that my mind was not there anymore. It was in Montreal, with my family, on the streets of the village where I live. I had been walking like a zombie for the last little while.

That is what happens at the beginning of mindfulness practice—you might notice that you are not paying attention, but you notice it only "after a while." With practice it becomes easier to catch the mind as it prepares to take a turn at the junction of Memory Lane.

I stopped and took a few moments to get back in touch with my breath. I continued walking at a slower pace, taking in the ohia blooms and the strawberry guava trees with their roots protruding above the soil. David Bader, the author of *Zen Judaism*, wrote: "Be here now, be somewhere else later. Is that so complicated?" But I was not finding it easy. I made a decision to stop walking every time I noticed I was in my thoughts for the rest of the hike. I was feeling a little bit like Henry David Thoreau when he wrote: "I am alarmed when it happens that I have walked a mile into the woods bodily, without getting there in spirit."

It is not that thoughts are "bad." But when body and mind are united, our walks inspire and refresh both. "I went to the woods because I wished to live deliberately, to front only the essential facts of life, and see if I could not learn what it had to teach, and not, when I came to die, discover that I had not lived." Thoreau's wisdom is grounded in the senses and in the here and now. It is not a one-sided, "cognitive-only" kind of wisdom.

When we walk to get something or to go somewhere, our purpose blinds us. We walk in a haze. We are not there yet, and we are not here either. Neither here nor there, we are in limbo.

Remember to be where you are until you get there. Then, when you are there, you will still be "here," except that now "here" has changed places. The trick is to always feel that you are "here." That way, you take "here" with you wherever you go. This is actually in accord with the facts—here and there are both matters of perspective.

Another way of practicing walking meditation is to feel that you are always at home. This is another meaning of "here." Home is where the heart is. Let your heart be where you are. Actually, scientifically, we are here now, we are not somewhere else. Here is where we always live. This is the practice of preserving the oneness of mind and body. Are you walking to your car? With every step, think, "I have arrived," not "I will arrive." You can say, "Here," with every step in order to remind yourself.

Here is a little mantra you can repeat:

A smile with every breath, a flower with every step,

I have already arrived, I'm already at home.

And when you get into your car, don't think, "I will soon arrive home."

Think instead, "I have already arrived, I am already at home." You are in the home in your heart.

Daydreaming as you walk, like I was doing in Oahu, is another way of not being present. When I noticed I was doing that, I stopped and got in touch with my breath. It is the body that breathes. When we are with our breath, we are with the body. And the body is always here. Then I put my attention in all my senses. The senses are also of the body. You can focus on the outer senses as well as the inner senses, such as the sensations of taking a step, the sensations of balancing, and the sensations that come from any muscular tension you are carrying with you.

Thich Nhat Hanh's meditation theme is a good one to walk with:

Peace is every step.

If you have something heavy on your mind, this "improved" version of the spiritual discussed in chapter 13 may come in handy:

I'm gonna lay down my burden, lay down my heavy load.

And give my heart back its wings.

The original words referred to physical burdens, but emotional burdens we carry can in fact be even heavier.

You can repeat the following mantra inspired by a Thich Nhat Hanh poem if you are preoccupied with a problem:

Breathing in, I come back to an island of peace in my heart.

Afterword

HERE AND NOW

"Here" and "Now" are twins
"Here" gives "Now" its color
and "Now" gives "Here" its perfume
neither can be boxed in
for they go on forever in all directions
"Here" may be sharp like the point of a needle
but there is a hand that holds the needle,
an eye that guides it
and a universe that supports it.
Mindfulness is a twinkle in the eye
a wink and a smile
that does not get caught in a lie
or in metaphysical blabber
it knows that behind that eye there is a liver
a spleen and a bladder.

Acknowledgments

I would like to express my deep gratitude to Thich Nhat Hanh for his confidence in appointing me a Dharma teacher in his lineage. This has allowed me to relate differently to the Buddhist teachings, and to take personal responsibility for it. Are our ideas and insights all ours, or do they also come from various sources, including our culture and our teachers? I have found the Buddhist tradition to be an abundant and constantly refreshing source of inspiration. I am indebted to the many teachers past and present who have kept that tradition alive.

A deep bow to the late Robert Aitken Roshi for giving me an early taste of Zen.

Thanks to all the people who attended my Mindfulness Meditation Training for Stress Reduction and Personal Growth courses or came to see me privately over the years. Your questions have goaded me to go deeper, and provided much material for this book. Participants in a course often express thanks to the person who is teaching. Here I would like to return the compliment and say how much I appreciate what I also learned during those sessions.

Thanks to Chantal Jacques and Valerie Legge for reading an early version of the manuscript and making valuable comments. Thanks also to my editor, Andrew Yackira, for guiding this project to completion in an easy and helpful manner, and all the staff at Tarcher/Penguin for help with various aspects of this project.

I would like to thank my partner, Suzanne Forest, for being herself.

I would like to thank flowers and trees for making the world more beautiful.

◆ ◆ ◆

Please contact Joseph Emet at josephemet@gmail.com for group and individual training in mindfulness practice.

31901055278388